RISING TO THE CHALLENGE
of the National Science Education Standards
The Processes of Science Inquiry

Dr. Karen Ostlund
Professor of Science
Southwest Texas State University
San Marcos, Texas

Sheryl Mercier
Intermediate Elementary Teacher
Fresno Unified School District
Fresno, California

ISBN 0-9658768-0-2

S & K Associates
Fresno, California

RISING TO THE CHALLENGE
of the National Science Education Standards
The Processes of Science Inquiry

This book was set in Tekton by S & K Associates.
The authors and editors were Karen Ostlund and Sheryl Mercier.
The illustrations were done by Sheryl Mercier.
Printed in the United States of America.

How Do We Meet the Challenges of the National Science Education Standards?

The Science Standards state that as a result of activities in grades K-4 and 5-8, all students should develop abilities necessary to do scientific inquiry and develop understandings about scientific inquiry.

The 36 investigative activities in this book are designed for students of the intermediate grades of 4th-8th to participate in science as inquiry as they investigate everyday objects and events -sea shells, rocks, and sound.

This is our first book created to assist educators in the teaching and application of the processes of inquiry : Observing, Communicating, Classifying, Measuring, Inferring, Predicting, Defining Operationally, Making Models, and Investigating.

We have used these activities with our own students and enjoyed enthusiasm and success. We wish the same for you and your students.

Karen Ostlund
Sheryl Mercier

Table of Contents

Rocks- Making Connections

Sound- Making Connections

Putting it All Together: A Science Fair Project

Assessment Strategies

THE PROCESSES OF INQUIRY

OBSERVING

Observing involves using one or more of the senses (seeing, hearing, smelling, tasting or touching) to find out about objects and/or events. Observations can be enhanced by using instruments such as hand lenses, microscopes, stethoscopes, etc. Observations must be communicated in order to assess them; therefore, one problem in assessment is that students can't communicate but they can observe. Another problem in communicating observations is that students make inferences (see below) instead of observations. For example, students may observe a bee flying toward a flower. They may infer that the flower smells good to the bee. An observation is a fact learned directly through the senses and not an interpretation or explanation of what is observed.

COMMUNICATING

Communicating is a method of giving or exchanging information from one person to another person. Communication is a two-way street, i.e., someone has to communicate in such a way that someone else can interpret it accurately. Examples include: oral communication or written communication such as using or making drawings, diagrams, pictures, photographs, maps, and symbols; constructing tables, charts, and graphs; or writing reports. Until something is communicated, it isn't learned.

CLASSIFYING

Classifying begins with observing similarities and differences among objects and/or events in order to group things according to a scheme. Classifying objects and events helps to put order in our lives. This helps us to see the relationships among things. The steps in classifying include: (1) comparing and contrasting objects and events to find likenesses and differences in order to find common characteristics among things; (2) the common characteristics are used to organize objects and events; (3) the objects and events are grouped according to these characteristics; and (4) the groups are labeled with a term or phrase that expresses the common characteristics of the objects or events in the group.

ESTIMATING & MEASURING

These skills go together since in order to develop measurement skills, it is important to have a frame of reference which is achieved through estimating before measuring. Measurements are quantitative (a number is involved) observations using standardized measuring tools such as rulers, balances, graduated cylinders, protractors, thermometers, stopwatches, etc. or nonstandardized objects like paper clips, cups, etc. These observations may be about area, length, volume, angle, temperature, time, force, mass, density, speed, etc. Accuracy is dependent on the nature of the measurement tool and the way it is used. Precision is the agreement among observed values in repeated measurements. It is not only important to improve the accuracy of measurements, but to devise instruments and techniques that will decrease the possible errors (precision) and also be as close as possible to the true value.

INFERRING

When you observe, you use the senses to collect information about objects and events. Inferences are always based on observations. When you infer, you draw a conclusion based on information not directly observed. Inferring requires evaluation and judgment based on past experiences. From these experiences, you learn to recognize patterns and expect the patterns to recur under the same conditions. For example, you observe a black car in the sun (your observations are the car is black and the sun is shining on it). You might infer that the car is hot. This is an inference because you did not directly observe the car by touching it but past experience has lead to the conclusion that the car is probably hot if it is black and the sun is shining on it.

PREDICTING

Predictions are always based on prior knowledge gained through experiences or data that is collected. A prediction is not a *wild guess* - it is based on observations and inferences. A prediction differs from a wild guess in that a wild guess is not based on evidence. A prediction is an *educated guess* about what will happen in the future. To predict accurately, you need to make careful observations and inferences about the relationships between observed events. Once made, predictions can be tested to determine their validity. After predictions have been tested, you can change or modify inferences on the basis of new data. When all of the evidence has been accumulated, you can draw conclusions about the way things work.

DEFINING OPERATIONALLY

An operational definition is a definition of an object or event based on your experiences with it. For example, after making a complete circuit, you might define a circuit as "a bulb, battery, and light arranged so the bulb lights up." I like to have students look up the definition of the concept in a science book and write the "book definition." When students compare their operational definition with the book definition, I think they gain a better understanding of the concept. An operational definition should be thought of as a "doing definition." Also, when you do an investigation, you must operationally define your variables (what you will change and what you will observe or measure).

MAKING MODELS

Making models involves developing a physical or conceptual representation to explain an idea, object, or event. Physical models can be made from clay, paper, boxes, straws, toothpicks, etc. Conceptual models can be making a diagram, cross-section, map, formula, etc. Anything that is not real but is a representation of an actual thing can be called a model. Using models helps develop abstract thinking as you learn to picture something in your mind after becoming familiar with it. Models should be compared to reality by noting similarities and differences between the model and the actual thing.

INVESTIGATING

HYPOTHESIZING - A hypothesis is a testable statement that answers a question about the way things work. Therefore, before a hypothesis can be stated, there should be a problem to be solved or a question to be answered. Then a hypothesis is stated in terms of an If. . . .then statement, i.e., If I do this, then I will observe that. This is a testable statement; I can do this and see if I observe that. This statement tells us about the relationship between the manipulated variable (what you will do) and the responding variable (what you will observe). It's all right to find out that your investigation does not support your hypothesis. Sometimes it's just as important to find out that things don't work the way you think they do as it is to find out that they do work that way.

COLLECTING DATA - Collecting data involves systematically collecting observations and measurements. The information can be collected in a data table, graph, log book, etc. Records of observations and measurements should be accurate and clear. As you collect data you should (1) describe the conditions under which the observations or measurements were made; (2) use tables and graphs to communicate data in an organized way; and (3) record information in detail, quantifying (giving a number) the information when possible.

MAKING A GRAPH - A graph is a diagram that organizes information or data. This information can often be communicated more easily with a picture instead of using the spoken or written word. Graphs are useful for comparing things. Bar and line graphs show relationships among the quantities collected. Bar graphs are used to show discrete objects or events such as different brands of paper towels or bubble solutions or trials. Line graphs are used to show continuous sets such as time, force, mass, length, etc. Circle graphs show the relative sizes of the parts that make up the whole. All graphs should have a title and be correctly labeled. Bar and line graphs are made with two main lines of reference called axes. The two axes of a graph often meet at zero. The manipulated or independent variable (what you change) is written along the horizontal axis and the responding or dependent variable (what you observe or measure) is written along the vertical axis.

INTERPRETING DATA - Interpreting data involves reading and understanding a table, graph, diagram, map, etc. This includes being able to explain the information presented and using the information to answer questions. Two basic processes are combined in interpreting data: (1) using numbers or symbols and (2) drawing conclusions. When you interpret data, you often perceive patterns in the information and express those patterns as a conclusion. For example, graphs can be used to make predictions by interpolating and extrapolating. If the observed values reveal a regular pattern, interpolation can be used to predict values that are in between the data points shown in the graph. Extrapolation can be used to predict values that extend beyond the range of data collected.

CONTROLLING VARIABLES - Variables are all the factors that can make a difference in an investigation. There are three types of variables: (1) manipulated (independent) variables, (2) responding (dependent) variables, and (3) controlled (constant) variables. You should (1) manipulate or change only one variable in a systematic way (manipulated variable); (2) measure any changes in the results (responding variable); and (3) control all other variables so they are the same (constant).

Cooperative/Collaborative Learning Groups

Cooperative learning involves students working together in small groups to help one another master skills and subject matter content. Research indicates that using cooperative group instructional strategies increases student achievement and social skill acquisition (Johnson, 1986). Developing social skills is an important prerequisite for academic learning since achievement will improve as students become more effective in working with each other. It is within cooperative group situations where there is academic material that must be mastered that social skills become most relevant. One of the most important advantages of cooperative learning tasks is that social skills are required, used, reinforced, and mastered.

We are not born with instinctive behaviors that help us interact in socially acceptable ways the first time we are placed in a situation in which we make contact with others. If we expect students to work together, we must teach them how to use social skills when working together just as purposefully and precisely as academic skills are taught. The acquisition of social skills is essential for building and maintaining an enduring family, a successful career, and lasting friendships. Therefore, learning in the context of cooperative groups requires students to develop and use the social skills that will be necessary for leading fruitful and fulfilling lives as adults.

How can student social skill acquisition be assessed in the context of cooperative learning?

The purpose of assessment has important implications for what information is collected and how it is gathered. Assessment involves many different ways of gathering information about students in order to plan instruction at a challenging but developmentally appropriate level for pupils. What are the social skills that should be assessed? How should these social skills be assessed? These are the questions this section attempts to answer.

What social skills should be assessed in cooperative learning groups?
The social skills listed below are divided into three categories: **(1) cluster skills** which help students form a group; **(2) task skills** which help the group complete the task; and **(3) camaraderie skills** which help group members like each other when the task is finished.

The **cluster skills** facilitate moving into groups quickly and quietly as well as beginning the group activity. The **task skills** have a content focus and help the group meet its subject matter objective as well as helping the group work effectively to create a high quality product. Task skills begin with skills that help groups manage completing the task, through skills that maximize the mastery and retention of the material, to skills that build deeper level understanding through the use of critical thinking skills. The **camaraderie skills** help students feel better about themselves, each other, and the group to build group cohesiveness and stability. The overall goal of social skill acquisition is positive, on-task students who enjoy their time together, care about each other, and produce high quality work.

Social Skills List

Cluster Skills

- Move into groups quietly.
- Stay with your group.
- Use quiet voices.
- Address people in your group by name.
- Look at the speaker.
- Listen actively.
- Look at the group's paper or project.
- Keep hands and feet to self.
- Share materials.
- Take turns.
- Encourage everyone to participate.
- Contribute ideas.

Camaraderie Skills

- Avoid put-downs.
- Give each member of your group a compliment.
- Express support and acceptance verbally and/or nonverbally.
- Express warmth and liking (toward group members and group).
- Describe feelings when appropriate.
- Energize the group with humor, ideas, or enthusiasm.
- Relieve tension by joking.
- Criticize ideas without criticizing people.

Task Skills

- Ask questions.
- Ask for help.
- Ask for clarification.
- Offer to explain or clarify.
- Check for understanding.
- Review the instructions
- State and/or restate the purpose of the assignment.
- Set or call attention to time limits.
- Offer procedures on how to most effectively do the task.
- Paraphrase other members' contributions.
- Clarify other members' contributions.
- Allow each person to speak once before speaking again.
- Summarize the material aloud.
- Pursue accuracy by correcting and/or adding to summaries.
- Seek elaboration by relating to other learning or knowledge.
- Search for clever ways of remembering ideas and facts.
- Encourage vocalization of other members' reasoning processes.
- Ask other members to plan out loud how to solve a problem or make a decision.
- Differentiate when there is disagreement.
- Integrate different ideas into a single position.
- Listen to all ideas before reaching consensus.

- Ask for justification of others' conclusions or ideas.
- Extend other members' answers or conclusions.
- Probe by asking in-depth questions that lead to deeper analysis.
- Generate further answers.
- Test reality by checking the group's work against instructions.

It is best to stress only **one** social skill each time a group engages in a cooperative group activity. The social skill should be determined by observing the operation of the groups to pick out behaviors which are not constructive to effective functioning by the group as a whole or individual group members. Once a skill has been identified which is appropriate for the cooperative group activity and the social development of the students, the teacher can explain, model, and elicit other examples of appropriate behaviors for the specific skill. For example, when teaching students to use quiet voices, the teacher could ask the students to place several fingers on their neck over the vocal chords, say something out loud to feel the vibration produced by the vocal chords, and then whisper something to feel that there is almost no vibration in the vocal chords.

When teaching students to encourage everyone to participate, each group member could be given counting chips of a different color which would be placed in the center of the group's work space each time someone encouraged another group member to participate. The different colored chips could be counted at the end of the activity to determine how many times each group member engaged in this behavior. The counting chips could be used again to teach students to allow each person to speak once before speaking again. This time each group member would receive one counter which would be used to take turns talking. When someone talks, s/he would place a counter in the middle of the group's work space and would not speak again until all four counters are in the center at which point the counters would be distributed back to each group member to used when talking again.

Establishing the goals for the cooperative classroom is a prerequisite to setting up cooperative learning activities. The expectations must be made clear and explicit so that complex tasks, such as using higher level collaborative skills becomes automatic. These three expectations are effective in establishing the goals in a cooperative classroom:

1. **Help me teach.**
2. **Help others' learn.**
3. **Be prepared to learn.**

The goals for the cooperative classroom determine the classroom rules which need to be observed in order to reach those goals. Classroom rules should be limited and stated in a positive manner. Establishing the norm behaviors expected in every cooperative learning activity is the first step in setting up assessment of the social skill behaviors. The following norm behaviors are effective in establishing the protocol for a cooperative classroom:

1. **Listen.**
2. **Be responsible for yourself.**
3. **Respect others.**
4. **Stay on task.**

Inappropriate behaviors that are not conducive to group functioning can be addressed by referring to these expectations. The first expectation, *Listen*, stops any talking when the teacher or any other person in the group is talking because one cannot listen and talk at the same time. The second expectation encourages each student to take responsibility for his/her behavior such as following directions, bringing required materials to class, and being seated and prepared to learn when the class begins. The third expectation takes care of one student interfering with another student with physical and/or verbal contact. Finally, the last expectation, addresses any off task behavior such as talking about what's for lunch or engaging in manipulating materials in an inappropriate manner.

How should social skills be assessed? Since the purpose of assessment has important implications for what information is collected and how it is gathered, assessment can involve many different ways of gathering information about students. One method of assessing students working in cooperative groups is to provide each group with a "ruler" such as the one shown below:

+5	+4	+3	+2	+1	0	-1	-2	-3	-4	-5

Names :_____   _____

_____   _____

Cooperative group members place this "ruler" in the center of their work space and put their names on it. This method of assessment awards five bonus points to each group engaging in the norm behaviors listed above and practicing the designated social skill for the particular cooperative group activity. The teacher monitors students' behavior when the cooperative groups start working. When a group is not engaging in the appropriate social skills, the teacher explains which behavior the students need to exhibit and demonstrates how to perform the social skill. The teacher crosses out the **+5** on the "ruler" so the group now has four bonus points for the activity. This method of assessing social skills shifts the responsibility for engaging in appropriate behavior from the teacher to the group members. The bonus points may be used in a variety of ways to reward each group for appropriate social skill behaviors: extra credit on the cooperative group assignment, viewing a special science video, participating in a demonstration for the class, etc.

Some reporting systems require that students be graded for "effort" or "citizenship" as well as mastery of the subject matter content. In this case, the teacher may choose to use a "ruler" like the one shown on the following page to grade the social skill behaviors that lead to demonstrating nebulous behaviors like "effort" or "citizenship."

105	100	95	90	85	80	75	70	65	60	55	
	50	45	40	35	30	25	20	15	10	5	0

Names : _____   _____

_____   _____

This assessment instrument would be used in the same manner as the "bonus point ruler" shown before. However, the students would be awarded a percentage score for appropriate social skill behaviors exhibited in the cooperative group activity which would be the highest number not crossed out. These scores could be averaged to derive a grade for "effort" or "citizenship." Notice that this assessment instrument awards a bonus percentage of 105 for appropriate norm behaviors in cooperative learning groups.

Some observations that have been made about using this method for assessing social skill development include the observance that a teacher seldom has to cross out more than one or two numbers on the "ruler." If students notice that the teacher is monitoring their group, they encourage each other to exhibit appropriate social skills. In some situations **one** particular student in a cooperative group may lack basic social skills. After several attempts are made by the teacher to encourage the other members of the group to provide constructive support for the student to engage in appropriate behaviors, it may be necessary to give that particular student his/her own individual "ruler" while the rest of the group continues to use a group "ruler." Generally, the use of the "ruler" is not an ongoing process of assessment throughout the entire school year. It is effective at the beginning of the year for getting started with assessing social skill behaviors in cooperative groups. However, after four to six weeks, students are usually exhibiting effective working relationships and it might not be necessary to use the instrument to award points/scores to each group. Social skill development sometimes retrogrades in the middle of the school year; so teachers might want to use the "rulers" for a few weeks to help remind students about expectations for behaviors.

One way to ensure interdependence is to assign complementary and interconnected roles to group members. Each group member is assigned a responsibility that the group needs to function. These include a **Principal Investigator** to manage the learning task and make sure everyone in the group understands what is being learned, a **Materials Manager** to distribute the needed materials for the group, a **Recorder/Reporter** to record and report information gathered to the other groups and the teacher, and a **Time Keeper** to keep track of time. Groups of six could include the additional roles of Encourager to reinforce members' contributions, and Observer to keep track of how well the group is collaborating.

The deck of playing cards can be used in assigning specific jobs. For example, the group member who holds the spade in each group is assigned the role of Principal Investigator; the person holding the club is assigned the job of Materials Manager; the person having the diamond is the Reporter/Recorder; and the group member with the heart is the Time Keeper. The job descriptions are listed below.

•Principal Investigator

The Principal Investigator is in charge of reading instructions, checking the activity results, asking informational questions of the teacher, and conducting group discussions about processes and results. Note: Only the "PI" from each group is allowed to ask the teacher informational questions after the group has discussed the assignment and has been unable to answer a question together. This limits the number of students asking questions about the assignment so that a teacher will have questions from only 6-8 students rather than 24-30 students. The "PI" either conducts the activity or assigns other group members to carry out the activity.

•Materials Manager

The Materials Manager is responsible for collecting and returning all materials and equipment for the science activity, assembling and operating equipment, and checking the activity results. The "MM" is the only student who will be out of his/her seat during the activity. After the lesson is introduced, directions are given, and questions are answered, the "MM" gathers the materials and returns to the group work station to set up the equipment for the activity. When group clean up is completed, the "MM" returns the materials and equipment to the supply area.

•Recorder / Reporter

The Recorder / Reporter is in charge of collecting the information and recording it on the worksheet, table, graph or other data collection instrument used in the activity. The "RR" in cooperation with the other members of the group is also responsible for certifying the results that are recorded by the group on the data sheets. If group members gather data individually, the "RR" collects the individual data sheets and hands them in to the teacher for the entire group. The "RR" is responsible for reporting the results of the group activity to the class. This can be an oral report given from his/her seat or a written report placed on a class summary chart on the chalk board. If the group has any special concerns or comments about the data collected, the "RR" is also responsible for giving this information before the discussion of results begins.

•Time Keeper

The Time Keeper is in charge of keeping track of time, watching for group safety, encouraging group members, monitoring the noise level, and checking the activity results. The "TK" may also observe and record interactions of the group.

One of the group members can even be assigned to monitor specific behaviors. For example, a group member may tally how many times each member of the group speaks in order to determine if everyone in the group is contributing ideas. The Time Keeper may be assigned the additional responsibility of noise monitor for the group by giving group members a signal when a quiet voice is not used. Student observers can be used to get even more extensive data on each group's functioning. However, try not to count too many different behaviors at one time. At first just keep track of who talks in each group to get a participation pattern for the groups. It is also a good idea for the teacher to collect notes on specific student behaviors so that the frequency data is extended. When it is obvious that group members lack certain collaborative skills they need in order to cooperate with each, the teacher will want to intervene in order to help the members learn these collaborative skills. However, teachers should not intervene any more than is absolutely necessary because groups can often work their way through their own problems (task and social skill) and acquire not only a solution, but also a method of solving similar problems in the future. The best time to teach cooperative skills is when the students need them. It is important that the cooperative skills be taught in the context of the class where they are going to be used, or are practiced in that setting, because transfer of skill learning from one situation to another cannot be assumed.

The **product** required from the group may be a report, a single set of answers that all members of the group agree to, the average of individual paper or test scores, or the number of group members reaching a specific criteria. Whatever the measure, the learning of group members needs to be evaluated by a criteria-referenced system. Besides assessing students on how well they learned the assigned concepts and information, group members should also receive feedback on how effectively they collaborated. Two grades may be given - one for achievement and one for collaborative behavior. Collaborative skills should focus both on members' contributions to each other's learning and to the maintenance of effective working relationships among group members.

Closure to the lesson can be provided by summarizing the major points in the lesson, asking students to recall ideas or give examples, or answering any final questions students have. At the end of the lesson, students should be able to summarize what they have learned and to understand where they will use it in future lessons. Besides assessing students on how well they learned the assigned material, group members should also receive feedback on how effectively they worked together. Two grades could be given for the activity: one for achievement and one for how well the group functioned (social skill behaviors). Social skills should focus both on members' contributions to each other's learning and to the maintenance of effective working relationships among group members. Provide closure to the cooperative learning activity by asking groups to state one social skill they performed well as they worked together and one social skill they need to work on the next time the group meets.

Using cooperative learning groups in science is an effective method of utilizing people and materials efficiently. In a class ranging in size from 24 to 30 students, only one-fourth of the materials you would normally need are required to involve students in hands-on science. Research indicates that students working cooperatively learn interpersonal skills, improve personal responsibility and learn concepts as well as or better than if they had worked on the science activity individually.

| +5 | +4 | +3 | +2 | +1 | 0 | -1 | -2 | -3 | -4 | -5 |

Names : _____   _____

_____   _____

| +5 | +4 | +3 | +2 | +1 | 0 | -1 | -2 | -3 | -4 | -5 |

Names : _____   _____

_____   _____

| +5 | +4 | +3 | +2 | +1 | 0 | -1 | -2 | -3 | -4 | -5 |

Names : _____   _____

_____   _____

| 105 | 100 | 95 | 90 | 85 | 80 | 75 | 70 | 65 | 60 | 55 |
| 50 | 45 | 40 | 35 | 30 | 25 | 20 | 15 | 10 | 5 | 0 |

Names : _____   _____

_____   _____

| 105 | 100 | 95 | 90 | 85 | 80 | 75 | 70 | 65 | 60 | 55 |
| 50 | 45 | 40 | 35 | 30 | 25 | 20 | 15 | 10 | 5 | 0 |

Names : _____   _____

_____   _____

| 105 | 100 | 95 | 90 | 85 | 80 | 75 | 70 | 65 | 60 | 55 |
| 50 | 45 | 40 | 35 | 30 | 25 | 20 | 15 | 10 | 5 | 0 |

Names : _____   _____

_____   _____

Responsibility Role Cards. Cut on solid lines and fold.

Principal Investigator

Professor: _____

1. Read instructions.
2. Lead group discussions.
3. Ask questions of the teacher.
4. Ensure participation of all group members.

Principal Investigator

Materials Manager

Professor: _____

1. Collect and return equipment.
2. Manage operation of equipment.
3. Ensure safe use of equipment.
4. Manage fair use of equipment.

Materials Manager

Time Keeper

Professor: _____

1. Monitor time.
2. Keep group on task.
3. Watch for group safety.
4. Encourage group members.

Time Keeper

Recorder Reporter

Professor: _____

1. Record data on group work.
2. Write activity results on class charts.
3. Report findings to the class.
4. Report all results fairly.

Recorder / Reporter

Introducing the Processes of Inquiry
Overhead Transparencies-Teaching Tips

The one page activity sheets that follow are designed as overhead transparencies for your use in directing students' introduction to the inquiry skills. Use the short activities to experience and discuss each skill as a guided whole group lesson. Allow time for metacognition (thinking about their thinking) of the steps they used to come to conclusions. Teaching tips for each activity are given below.

Observing

Materials: wintergreen lifesaver, or assorted candies

Directions: Ask students to name their five senses and identify how they use each sense. Give students a wintergreen lifesaver and ask them to use as many senses as they can to make observations about the lifesaver. Have students share their observations with their team of four. The team with the longest list is the most observant!

Communicating

Materials: Scotch Magic® tape, pencil

Directions: Ask student to list of ways they communicate. Make a master list on the chalkboard. Ask why it is important to communicate. Then display the overhead. Have students scribble on a piece of scratch paper with a pencil, rub their left thumbs on it, put tape on their thumbs to lift the prints, and stick the tape on a piece of paper to see their thumbprints. Ask students to look at their thumbprints and describe them in detail using words and diagrams or drawings. Then have them read their descriptions to their teams. Other team members compare the description to see if they have a similar pattern. Then ask the entire class to compare thumbprints. Describe the arch-loop-whorl system of classifying fingerprints. Ask students to suggest ways of communicating class results. One possibility is to make a concrete graph using the pieces of tape with the thumbprints.

Classifying

Materials: trail mix or bean soup, or pasta, or nuts/nails/bolts or leaves

Directions: Display objects on the overhead and project their shadow on the screen. Model how to separate the objects into groups. Ask students how the objects are alike and how they are different. Then have students separate their sets of objects into groups based on similarities and differences.

Measuring

Materials: as many measuring tools as possible

Directions: Display the measuring tools on a table and model how to use them. For example, a transparent ruler can be used on the overhead to measure the volume of a box. Then have students measure the volume of a box. Go over the information and steps for measuring on the overhead. Students can practice by measuring objects in and around their desks.

Inferring

Materials: 2 plastic cups of "clear liquids" (water and vinegar)

Directions: Display 2 cups of clear liquids on the overhead so the light shines through them. Ask students to infer what the liquids could be (Sprite®, H$_2$O, salt water, sugar water, Crystal Light®, ammonia, cleaning fluid, Ivory® soap, 7-Up®, Jell-O® water, Karo® syrup). Manipulate the cups so students can observe how the liquids pour in order to eliminate some of the inferences. Add items to the liquids such as paper clips, food coloring, salt, sand, vinegar, baking soda, etc.

Predicting

Materials: ball that bounces, meter stick

Directions: Show a ball and have students guess how high the ball will bounce without prior observations. Then gather data by taping a meter stick to the wall in order to observe how high the ball bounces when dropped from various heights. Finally, have students predict how high the ball will bounce from other heights.

Defining Operationally

Materials: construct a pendulum using string and a weight (lifesaver, washer, etc.)

Directions: Have students observe the pendulum. Ask how you could get the pendulum to swing. Then ask students to define the period of the pendulum (i.e., one swing, back and forth). Explain that an operational definition tells what you do and what happens. It also describes what will be observed or measured.

Making Models

Materials: plastic resealable bag, water, balloon

Directions: Have students make a model of a cell using the plastic bag for the cell membrane, the water for the cytoplasm, and the balloon for the nucleus and small beans or seeds for mitochondria. Then ask students how the model differs from a real cell. Display the overhead and go over the information and steps for making models.

Investigating

Materials: water, 2 plastic cups, liquid soap or detergent, 2 pennies, 2 eye droppers

Directions: Ask students how many drops of water they can put on a penny before the water spills over. Then ask them if adding soap to the water will affect the number of drops of liquid that a penny will hold. Have students complete the steps listed on the overhead to conduct this investigation to find out if adding soap to water affects the number of drops a penny will hold. The soap breaks the force of attraction between the molecules by getting between the molecules. The surface tension of the water is broken and the penny will not hold as many drops of a solution of soap and water.

Learning Groups

OBSERVING

We observe when we use one or more of our senses to find out about objects, events, or living things. An observation is a fact learned directly through the senses.

Sight

Touch

Smell

Taste

I can use instruments to make more detailed observations.

magnifier

telescope

microscope

satellite

stethoscope

How do I make accurate observations?

1. Use as many senses as you can when you observe. Never taste unless you are told to taste something.

2. Think about how you can use your senses to obtain information about an object or event. Pick up an object, feel it, smell it.

3. Describe only what you observe directly with your senses.

4. Notice things that are changing. Include observations before, during and after the change.

© 1996 Mercier / Ostlund

COMMUNICATING

We communicate when we give or receive information. Precise language is needed for describing an observation, reporting a measurement or interpreting data.

How do I communicate?

1. Observe, then describe enough properties of an object or event so someone can identify it.

2. Describe changes in the properties of an object or event.

3. Describe and order changes in the properties of an object or event.

4. Use diagrams, charts, graphs, writing, speaking, visuals, and photos to communicate.

CLASSIFYING

We classify when we use observations to group objects or events according to similarities and differences. Classification schemes can be one-two-or multistage.

How are these alike and different?

size
luster
mass
shape
chemistry

We need a name for each group.

How do I classify?

1. Observe a set of objects or events. Think about their properties.

2. Divide the set into 2 or more groups based on one observable property.

3. Divide the group(s) on the basis of a second observable property.

4. Continue to divide the groups on the basis of observable properties.

5. Put the properties used into an outline or diagram.

MEASURING

We measure when we compare something to standard or nonstandard units. The basic units for measuring are length, mass and time. All units come from these three.

Direct Measurements:

Temperature: measure the length of a column of alcohol.

Force: measure the length of a stretched spring.

Area: measure the length and width and find the product. $l \times w = area$

Derived Measurements:

Volume: measure length, width and height and find the product. $l \times w \times h = V$

Speed: divide distance by time. $D \div t = s$

Density: divide mass by volume $V \div m = d$

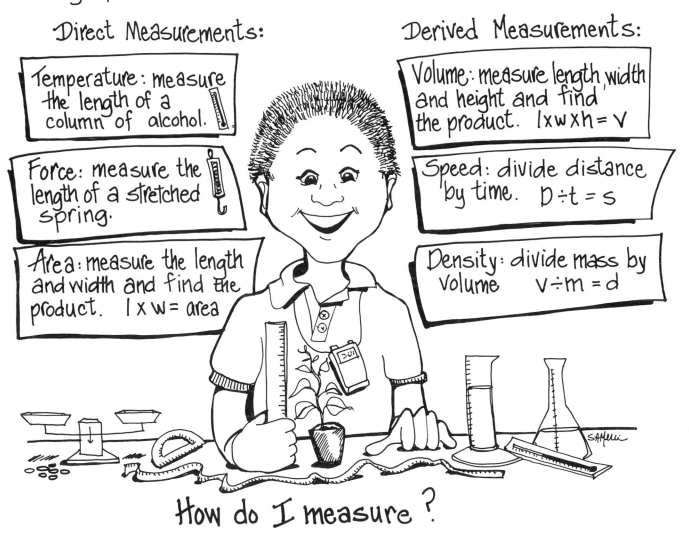

How do I measure?

1. Estimate the measurement.

2. Compare to standard or nonstandard units.

3. Be as accurate as possible.

4. Calculate for derived measurements.

INFERRING

We infer when we use our past experiences to draw conclusions and make explanations about events not directly observed.

Inferences are based on observations.

An observation is a personal experience obtained through one or more of the senses.

I can make more than one inference to explain an observation.

It looks like water....

It feels like water....

It pours like water....

How do I infer?

1. Make an observation of an object or event.

2. Use your past experiences. Think of several inferences.

3. Decide what new observations would support those inferences.

4. Make new observations to determine if each of the inferences is an acceptable explanation.

PREDICTING

We predict when we make a forecast about what will happen in the future. Predictions are based on prior knowledge gained through experiences and data that is collected.

Drop	Bounce
25	10
30	12
50	
75	
100	

How do I make accurate predictions?

1. Make observations and/or measurements. Recall past experiences.

2. Use your knowledge to search for patterns in the data. Make inferences.

3. Make predictions about future events. Use your inferences.

4. Test those predictions to determine validity.

5. After testing, revise predictions if necessary.

DEFINING OPERATIONALLY

We define operationally when we write a definition of an object or event based on our experiences with it. It is a doing definition.

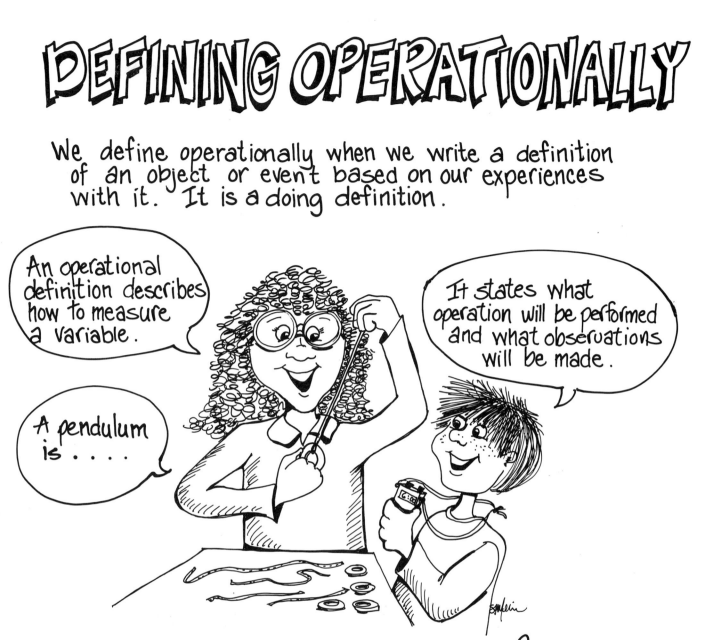

How do I write an operational definition?

1. Observe an object or event. Test or investigate.

2. Think about those observations.

3. Describe what you can do and what you can observe.

4. Write an definition that communicates what the object does.

MAKING MODELS

We make models when we develop a physical or conceptual representation to explain an idea, object or event. Anything that is not real but is a representation of an actual thing can be called a model.

How do I make a model?

1. Find out about an object or event.

2. Think about what you could do to represent the object or event.

3. Construct the model.

4. Compare your model to the actual object or event. How are they alike? different?

INVESTIGATING

How do I investigate?

1. State the question or problem you are investigating

2. Write an If.... then.... statement (hypothesis). that tells what you think the answer is to the question or problem.

3. Describe the design of the investigation.
   - the manipulated variable (what you will change and how you will change it)
   - the responding variable (what you will observe/measure)
   - the controlled variable (what you keep the same)

4. Carry out the investigation according to your design.

5. Report the data you collect in a table.

6. Construct a graph to show your data.

7. State the relationship you observed between the variables.

8. Compare your results to your hypothesis.

9. State if your hypothesis was supported or refuted by your investigation.

Shells - Making Connections

The Processes of Inquiry / Content Standards

Life Science Standards:
Levels K-4
- Characteristics of organisms

Levels 5-8
- Structure and function in living systems

In the following activities, students use the processes of inquiry to discover characteristics of organisms and structure and function in living systems.

Observe a Shell

Materials: seashell, tape measure, color crayons, pencils, or markers

Directions: Tell students that everyone is going to observe something that is often found on beaches. Have students ask questions that can be answered with "yes" or "no" to guess what they will observe today. Ask students to select and observe their seashell using the senses of sight, touch, smell, and hearing. Have them use a tape measure to make quantitative (numbers) observations. Encourage students to use as many descriptive words as possible when making qualitative (words) observations.

Connecting Content : Although seashells vary in pattern, size, and shape, they are all made by the animals that live inside them, and all grow outward. Snail-like shells are built like a spiral staircase, with the shell winding down around a central shaft. The nautilus shell is made differently from most shells. Each section of the spiral is sealed off as the animal moves out farther from the center. One of the most symmetrical seashells is the sundial. Its whorls grow in a continuous, even curve.

Communicating about Shells

Materials: seashells, color crayons, pencils, or markers

Directions: Place a set of seashells where all group members can observe the shells. Then have each group member pick a shell to observe and describe. Tell students not to touch the shell or indicate which one they have selected. The other members of the group should try to guess which shell each person is describing. Ask students to observe and describe their seashell in enough detail that other students can identify the seashell.

Connecting Content: Many mollusks pause between periods of growth, creating a shell of varying thicknesses. These growth rings can be seen in some shells, such as oysters, and are often so regular that they become a reliable means of identifying the species.

Classifying with Shells

Materials: seashells, color crayons, pencils, or markers

Directions : Divide a set of seashells into two groups based on one property; i.e., shape of shell. Ask students to guess the property you used to divide the shells into two groups. Then have students observe and divide their seashells into groups according to similarities and differences.

Connecting Content: Biologists divide mollusks into seven groups, called classes, but only some of them count as seashells. **Gastropods,** or univalves, have a single shell. Most have a coiled shell, although some (like limpets and slipper-shells) have a cap-shaped shell. Snails, periwinkles, whelks, and conches are gastropods.
Pelecypods, or bivalves, have two shells, or valves, hinged together. They include clams, oysters, and scallops.
Tusk shells, or scaphopods, look like elephants' tusks and are open at both ends. They bury themselves in the sand with only the narrow end sticking out to suck in water.
Chitons, or polyplacophora, have eight overlapping plates, attached to the back of the soft-bodied animal and bound together at the sides by a stretchy muscular band known as a girdle, which allows the animal to move over irregular surfaces. When a chiton is detached from its ground, it curls up to protect its soft body.

Measuring Shells

Materials: seashell, tape measure, balance, plastic cup and saucer, graduated cylinder

Directions: Ask students to estimate the circumference, mass, and volume of a seashell. Then demonstrate how to use a tape measure, balance, displacement cup, and graduated cylinder to measure the shell. Ask students to estimate measurements and then use a tape measure, balance, displacement cup, and graduated cylinder to measure their seashell. Use seashells that are large enough to break the surface tension of the water when finding the volume of their shell.

Connecting Content : As mollusks grow, the shell in which it lives grows. The soft creature creates the hard shell by depositing calcium carbonate onto a framework of protein, called conchiolin. The secretions are made by a sheet of soft tissue called the mantle, which is located between the shell and the inner organs that it encloses. If you examine the lip of a live shell, you can detect a thin, flexible layer of developing shell material. The shell is vulnerable at this point, so many mollusks have developed a trap door, called an operculum, to protect the exposed part of the body.

Inferring with Shells

Materials: seashell, tape measure, color crayons, pencils, or markers

Directions : Place a set of seashells so all members of the groups can observe them. Then give each group a piece of shell that is the same kind as one of the shells in their sets. Ask groups to compare the piece of shell to their set of shells to determine from which shell the piece came. Then give each student a piece of shell to observe and infer what it was like in its entirety before it was broken.

Connecting Content
The shape of the different sections, the color, and their overall size will help to identify gastropods. The point of the gastropod shell is called the spire. It was the first part formed. As the gastropod grew, it added a new whorl to the shell and moved into it. The number of whorls show how old the shell is. The outer lip of the body whorl gets thicker as the gastropod gets older. The largest section is called the body whorl. It is the last place the gastropod lived. The shape of the scars and the number of hinge teeth help to identify bivalves. The scar shows where the mantle muscles were attached. The beak is the first part of the shell to be formed. The growth lines that can be seen at the closed end of a bivalve shell show how big the shell was at different stages in the bivalve's life.

Predicting with Shells

Materials: bucket of seashells

Directions : Ask students to observe the bucket of shells and predict whether most of the shells are univalves (one shell) or bivalves (two shells). *Note: Show students an example of a univalve and a bivalve.* Explain to students how to use sampling techniques to determine the number of univalve and bivalve seashells in a bucket. Then ask them to predict the number of univalves and bivalves in the entire bucket based on their sampling.

Connecting Content

If you picked up a seashell from a beach, you are most likely to find the empty shell of a sea snail. Snails are mollusks known as *gastropods* or *univalve* shells. Gastropod is from Greek words for *stomach* and *foot*, and it is around the massive foot of a snail that all its important organs are found. Univalve describes the single shell, often coiled in a spiral shape. Like gastropods, *bivalves* are mollusks, but their shells are divided into two parts, or valves, that enclose and protect the soft body of the mollusk inside. The valves are connected by a rippled ridge or teeth that form a hinge which can be opened and closed by strong muscles and ligaments.

Defining Operationally

Materials: seashell, dictionary or science book

Directions: Ask students to list everything they have discovered about seashells. Then ask students to define *seashell* based on their experiences with seashells and then compare their definition with the definition in a dictionary or science book to determine similarities and differences.

Connecting Content : The word *shell* actually means a hard outer casing that encloses and protects a variety of things (fruit, baby birds, snails, crabs, etc.). A *seashell* is always a means of protection - against predators, mechanical damage, and extreme temperatures. See the information under **Classifying** for the groups of Mollusks that are seashells.

Making Models

Materials : seashell, Model Magic®, color crayons, pencils, or markers

Directions : Show students a model of something; i.e., car, airplane, globe, etc. Ask how the model is different from the actual object. Then have students use Model Magic® to make a model of their seashell. Ask them to compare their model to an actual shell to determine similarities and differences.

Connecting Content : Models of seashells seldom show how the organism carries on life processes. The gastropod is open at one end so that it can puts its head and foot out to feed and move about. A gastropod takes water in and out through its siphon which reaches the outside at the open end of the shell. Compared to the gastropods, bivalves do not lead very active lives. They are not able to extend very far out of their shells to crawl. Therefore, bivalves live embedded in sand and mud, or remain hidden in rock crevices, or attach themselves to a hard surface. Bivalves feed by opening their valves and filtering water through their gills to catch tiny creatures in the water.

Investigating Shells

Materials : seashells, eye dropper, graduated cylinder, water

Directions : Tell students that scientists conduct investigations to find out about the organism that made the seashell. This investigation will determine how the organism growing inside the shell affects the volume of the shell. Ask students to investigate the volume of water that different seashells will hold. Have them measure the volume and record their data in a chart and on a graph.

Connecting Content : Mollusks lay masses of eggs, because only a few will survive. The eggs hatch into larvae. The larvae begin to grow a shell. As the mollusk grows, its shell grows with it. The point of the gastropod shell, called the spire, was the first part formed. As the gastropod grew, it added a new whorl to the shell and moved into it. The number of whorls show how old the shell is. The outer lip of the body whorl gets thicker as the gastropod gets older. The largest section is called the body whorl. It is the last place the gastropod lived. In a bivalve, the beak is the first part of the shell to be formed. The growth lines that can be seen at the closed end of a bivalve shell show how big the shell was at different stages in the bivalve's life. Many oysters have growth rings on their top valves, like a sliced tree trunk.

Seashells

The scientific study of shells is conchology.

Seashells are the exoskeletons of small invertebrate animals called mollusks. The shell is the outside skeleton that supports and protects the soft slippery body of the mollusk. Shells range in size from a grain of sand to four foot, five hundred pound clam of the South Pacific Ocean. Some have beautiful shapes and bright colors while others are plain and colorless. Mollusk shells can be divided into five groups.

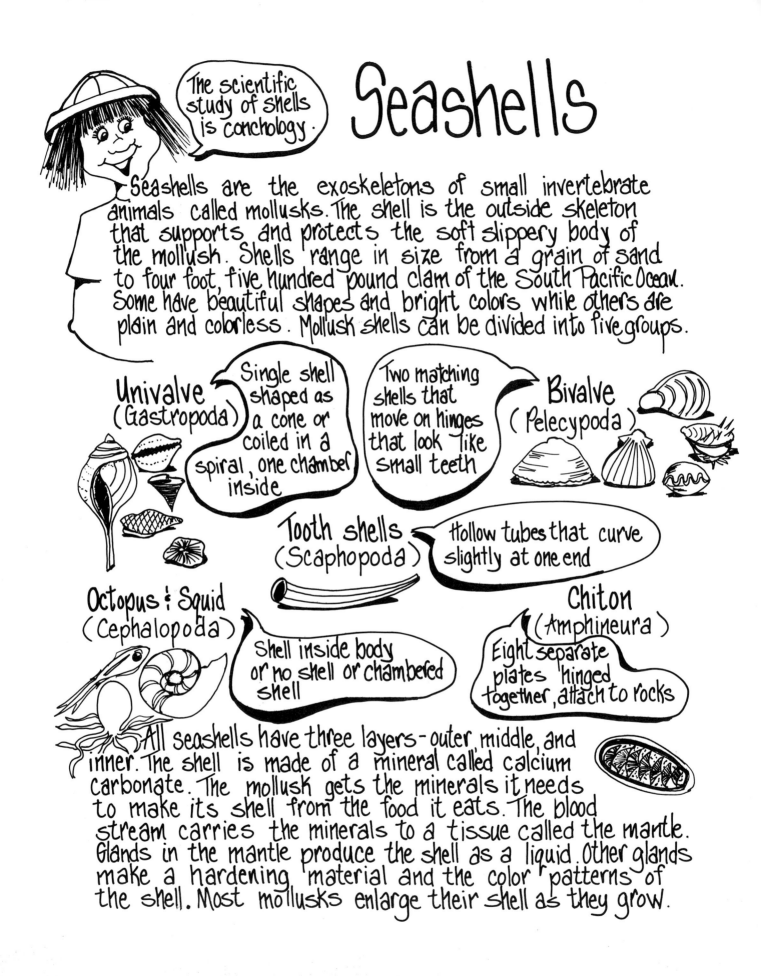

Univalve (Gastropoda)
Single shell shaped as a cone or coiled in a spiral, one chamber inside

Bivalve (Pelecypoda)
Two matching shells that move on hinges that look like small teeth

Tooth shells (Scaphopoda)
Hollow tubes that curve slightly at one end

Octopus & Squid (Cephalopoda)
Shell inside body or no shell or chambered shell

Chiton (Amphineura)
Eight separate plates hinged together, attach to rocks

All seashells have three layers - outer, middle, and inner. The shell is made of a mineral called calcium carbonate. The mollusk gets the minerals it needs to make its shell from the food it eats. The blood stream carries the minerals to a tissue called the mantle. Glands in the mantle produce the shell as a liquid. Other glands make a hardening material and the color patterns of the shell. Most mollusks enlarge their shell as they grow.

Observe a SHELL

1. Pick one seashell. Use your senses to observe and record its traits.

2. Trace the shell on the graph paper below.

3. Color in the details.

4. Use your senses to make a word bank that describes your shell.

Sight color shape pattern	Touch texture feel	Smell odor	Hearing drop & listen

5. Write a sentence that describes your shell.

Name: _____   Date: _____

Communicating about SHELLS

1. Use your senses to help you draw and describe your shell.

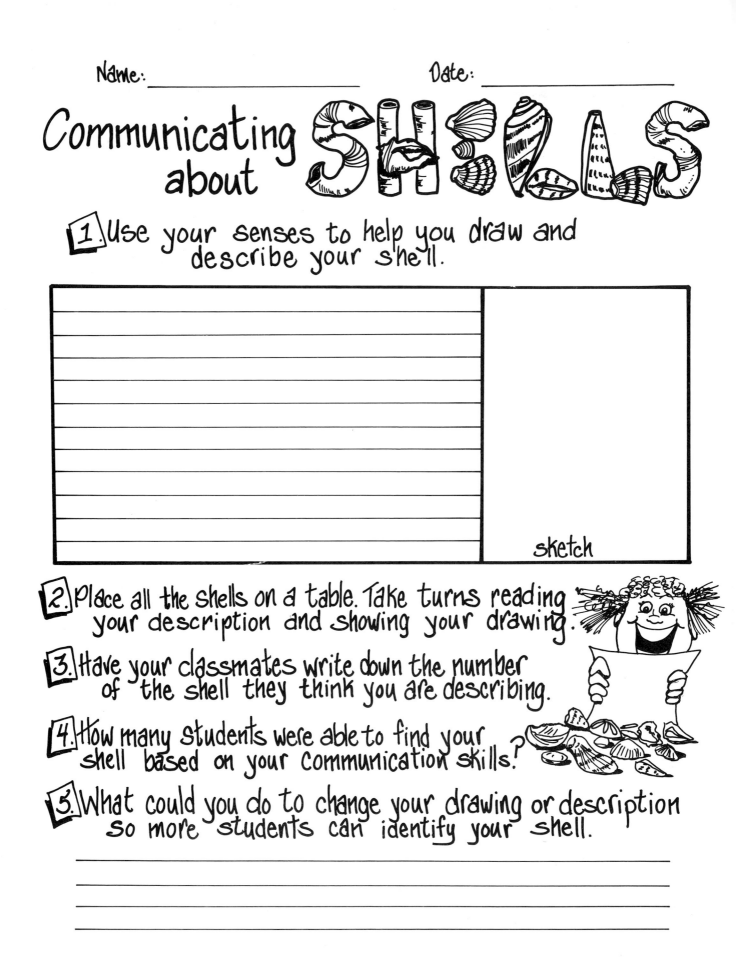

sketch

2. Place all the shells on a table. Take turns reading your description and showing your drawing.

3. Have your classmates write down the number of the shell they think you are describing.

4. How many students were able to find your shell based on your communication skills?

5. What could you do to change your drawing or description so more students can identify your shell.

_____

_____

_____

_____

Classifying with SHELLS

1. Observe and compare your set of shells. How are they alike? How are they different? Make a list.

Alike	Different

2. Divide your shells into 2 groups based on one of the properties you observed. Trace each shell into one of the groups. Color in the details.

Group 1: _____

Group 2: _____

3. Describe the steps you took to group your shells. _____

The ways the shells are alike and different are called properties.

density —
luster —
— color
— size
— shape

Scientists use properties to group and classify objects, events, and living things.

Name: _____ Date: _____

Measuring SHELLS

Estimate and then measure. Record.

1. LINEAR

	Estimate	Actual
Length		
Width at widest part		
Width at narrowest part		
Circumference at widest part		
Circumference at narrowest part		
Height from surface		

2. MASS

	Estimate	Actual
grams		

3. VOLUME

Fill cup. Put in shell. Catch spill.

	Estimate	Actual
milliliters or cubic centimeters		

Pour and measure spilled water.

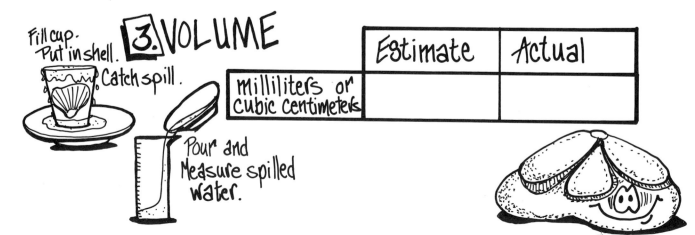

37

Name: _____ Date: _____

Inferring with SHELLS

1. Observe the broken shell. What do you think the whole shell looked like?

2. Trace the broken shell below. Complete the drawing with what you think the rest of the shell looked like.

3. Add details with color.

4. Explain your drawing. _____
_____
_____
_____
_____

Name: _____ Date: _____

Predicting with SHELLS

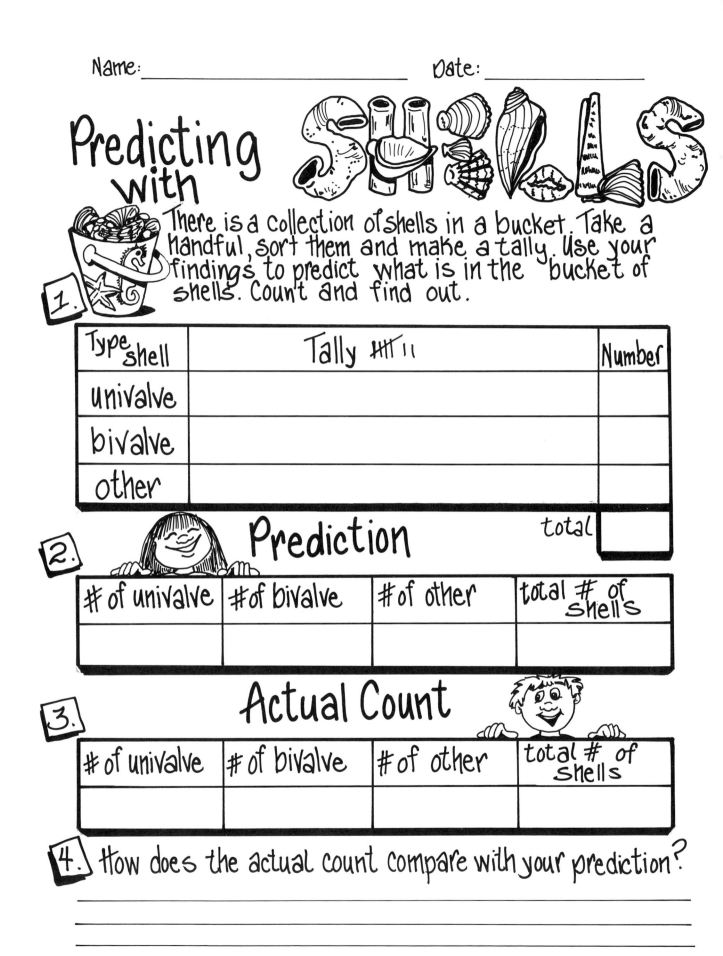

1. There is a collection of shells in a bucket. Take a handful, sort them and make a tally. Use your findings to predict what is in the bucket of shells. Count and find out.

Type shell	Tally ⲐⲐ‖	Number
univalve		
bivalve		
other		
	total	

2. Prediction

# of univalve	# of bivalve	# of other	total # of shells

3. Actual Count

# of univalve	# of bivalve	# of other	total # of shells

4. How does the actual count compare with your prediction?

_____

_____

Name_____ Date_____

Defining Operationally

1. You have experienced activities with seashells. Write a definition for seashells based on your experiences.

_____

_____

_____

_____

2. Find the definition of seashell in the dictionary or a science book and record it below.

_____

_____

_____

_____

3. How is your definition like this definition?

_____

_____

_____

4. How does it differ from this definition?

_____

_____

_____

Making Models

Use modeling compound to make a physical representation of a shell

1. Make careful observations — weight — color

Size
length width height

shape
coiled
oval round

texture
smooth
rough

2. After your model dries, add colors and patterns to your shell.

3. Analyze your model. How does your model compare to the real shell?

_____

_____

_____

_____

4. What do you need to make a more accurate model?

_____

_____

5. What could you use to represent the mollusk inside the shell?

_____

Name: _____ Date: _____

Investigating SHELLS

Problem: Which shell has the most space for the soft bodied mollusk that lived inside?

Hypothesis: If a shell has more space inside, then it will hold more water.

1. Observe 5 shells. Predict which one will hold the most water. Sketch them in order from most space to least space.

Most →   Least

#_____   #_____   #_____   #_____   #_____

2. Measure and record the amount of water each shell holds.

Graph:

Shell #	Water

#_____ / #_____ / #_____ / #_____ / #_____

3. How do your results compare with your prediction?
_____

4. Conclusion: _____
_____

Rocks - Making Connections

The Processes of Inquiry / Content Standards

Earth and Space Science Standards:

Levels K-4
- Properties of earth materials

Levels 5-8
- Structure of the earth system

In the following activities, students use the processes of inquiry to discover properties of earth materials and structure of the earth system.

Observing Rocks

Materials: rock, plastic cup of water, hand lens, color crayons, pencils, or markers

Directions: Pick up a rock and put it in your hand. Then tell students that you have something in your hand and invite them to guess what it is by asking questions that can be answered with a "yes" or "no." After students have guessed that you are holding a rock, ask them to describe rocks they have observed. Point out differences in the descriptions; i.e., rocks can be dark, light, smooth, rough, large, small, shiny, dull, etc. Then have students observe and draw their rock dry and wet. Then ask them to compare the appearance of the rock dry and wet. Finally, have them describe the texture of their rock.

Connecting Content: Observing a rock can give clues to its identity. Rocks are made of minerals so color can be misleading because the same mineral can come in many colors. But looking at luster (the way minerals in the rock reflect light) can be more useful. The minerals can be metallic (shiny like metal), vitreous (glistening like broken glass), or dull. A rock can be translucent (you can see light through it, or completely opaque (you can't see anything at all through it). Examining a rock with a hand lens is the best way to see the mineral content.

Communicating about Rocks

Materials: rock, hand lens, reference book on rocks

Directions : Place a set of rocks where all group members can observe the rocks. Then have each group member pick a rock to observe and describe. Tell students not to touch the rock or indicate which one they have selected. The other members of the group should try to guess which rock each person is describing. Then ask students to prepare a poster session to teach others about their rock.

Connecting Content : Minerals are the building blocks of rocks. Without rocks to supply us with minerals, we would not have bricks for building, metals for machines, oil to burn, or gems for jewelry. Only a few of the more than one hundred elements make up almost all of the compounds called minerals. Most rocks are composed of only eight of the chemical elements (oxygen, silicon, aluminum, iron, calcium, magnesium, sodium, and potassium). Silicon and oxygen combine in silicates which make up 75% of the Earth's rocks. Most minerals are crystalline; that is, the atoms that make up the crystals are arranged in an orderly fashion.

The Earth's crust is made from: 64.7% dark igneous (42.7% basalt) and light igneous (22.0% granite); 27.4% metamorphic (21.4% gneiss, 5.1% schist, and 0.9% marble); and 7.9% sedimentary (4.2% shale, 2.0% limestone, and 1.7% sandstone).

Classifying with Rocks

Materials: 8 rocks, color crayons, pencils, or markers

Directions : Explain how to use a multistage classification system to organize 8 rocks. Begin by asking students to divide the rocks into two groups; i.e., dark and light rocks. *Note: Pick a property so that you have two groups of four rocks.* Then ask students to divided each of these groups into two groups; i.e., smooth and rough. *Note: Pick a property so that you have four groups of two rocks.* Finally, ask students to divide the groups one more time; i.e., shiny an dull. *Note: Each rock should be by itself at this stage.* Remind students to think about the properties used to sort the rocks so that each rock ends up in its own box at the bottom of the page.

Connecting Content:
Clastic sedimentary rocks can be classified as *large-grained* (sandstone), *medium-grained* (sandstone), *fine-grained* (shale), or *mixed-grained* (conglomerate). Chemical sedimentary rocks can be classified as *carbonates* (limestone, chalk, dolomite), *silica* (agate, jasper, flint), or *other* (coal, rock salt, gypsum).

Igneous rocks can be classified as *plutonic* (coarse crystals), such as granite, diorite, and gabbro; *volcanic* (fine crystals) such as rhyolite, andesite, and basalt; or *pyroclastic* (shot from volcanoes), such as obsidian and pumice.

Metamorphic rocks can be classified as *massive*, (random nonrepeating texture) such as quartzite and marble, *foliated*, (ordered repeating texture) such as schist and gneiss, or *other* such as slate and serpentinite.

Measuring Rocks

Materials: 2 rocks, tape measure, balance, plastic cup and saucer, graduated cylinder

Directions: Ask students to estimate the circumference, mass, and volume of a rock. Then demonstrate how to use a tape measure, balance, displacement cup, and graduated cylinder to measure the rock. Ask students to select a rock, estimate measurements, and use a tape measure, balance, displacement cup, and graduated cylinder to measure their rocks. Use rocks that are large enough to break the surface tension of the water when finding the volume of their rock. Have students draw and label a diagram to show the measurements of their rocks.

Connecting Content: The elements in the periodic table are divided into metals and nonmetals (metalloids are between the two groups). Therefore, the minerals in rocks contain elements that are metals or nonmetals. Metals are usually more dense than nonmetals. The density of an irregular rock can be measured by water displacement.

Inferring about Rocks

Materials: rock, rock chart

Directions: Tell students that one way rocks are classified is according to how they were formed. Igneous rocks are formed from molten earth materials. Sedimentary rocks are formed from earth materials that are broken down and deposited as sediments. Metamorphic rocks are igneous, sedimentary, or metamorphic rocks that have changed due to heat and/or pressure. Have students observe their rock and compare it to the descriptions of metamorphic, sedimentary, and igneous rocks on the rock chart. Then ask them to infer what kind of rock they have.

Connecting Content: The longer it takes **igneous** rock to cool, the larger the crystals or grains in the rock. There are three main types of igneous rocks: *plutonic,* (coarse crystals), such as granite, which cool slowly in massive intrusions deep underground; *volcanic* (fine crystals), such as basalt, formed by lava spewed onto the surface of the Earth by volcanoes and cooled quickly; and *pyroclastic,* shot from volcanoes, such as obsidian and pumice.

Metamorphic rocks are tough and crystalline. There are two different types of metamorphism: *contact* and *regional. Contact* metamorphism occurs when rocks are remade by the heat of a volcanic intrusion. Sandstone changes to hard, close-grained metaquartzite; pure limestone becomes brilliant white marble; and mudstone and shale turn into dark hornfels close to the intrusion, while farther away they may become spotted rocks. *Regional* metamorphism occurs when rock is crushed beneath a range of mountains that develop between colliding continental plates. The enormous pressure gives rocks a distinctive foliated (banded) texture.

Sedimentary rocks can be clastic, or organic and chemical. The most common clastic rocks are conglomerate, sandstone, siltstone, and shale. Conglomerate is a solid mass of rounded pebbles. Sandstone is made from grains of quartz sand held together by silica or calcite. Siltstone is made of even finer grains; and shale is a smooth rock made from brittle flakes of compacted clay. The most common organic and chemical sedimentary rocks are limestones which are rich in calcium compounds. These include shell limestones, made from fragments of seashells, and chalk, made from the skeletons of microscopic sea creatures called coccoliths. Coal is made from the remains of swampy forests.

Predicting with Rocks

Materials: 100 ml each of sand, pebbles, and gravel, plastic container with lid, water, colored crayons, pencils or markers

Directions: Ask students to describe the differences in the three earth materials: sand, pebbles, and gravel. Point out that the main difference is the size of the particles. Ask students which earth material would be the heaviest (pebbles) and the lightest(sand). Ask students what would happen if these earth materials were put in water. (They would sink with the pebbles on the bottom since they are heavier.) Then have students put 100 ml of sand and pebbles into a plastic container, add water, shake it, and observe the results. Ask them to add 100 ml each of sand, pebbles, and gravel and predict the results that would be obtained after shaking the container.

Connecting Content: Most sedimentary rocks are "clastic" (formed from fragments of rock that are worn away by the weather and washed into the sea by rivers). Moving water is like a sieve, sorting rock fragments by size as it carries smaller grains farther and faster. Sedimentary rocks can be divided into three different groups according to grain size: large-grained *rudites* such as conglomerates and breccias; medium-grained *arenites* such as sandstones; and fine-grained *lutites* such as shale and clay. Some rocks are *turbidites*, such as graywackes, contain a mixture of grain sizes but the rock is banded into layers in which grains are graded in size from top to bottom. This is called "graded bedding." It is caused by the grains settling out of the water at slightly different rates as this activity demonstrates. Heavier grains sink more quickly, so the big grains tend to end up at the bottom. As this settling process can happen again and again, graywackes contain many bands of grains graded in this way.

Defining Operationally

Materials: rock, dictionary or science reference book

Directions: Ask students to list everything they have discovered about rocks. Then have students define *rock* based on their experiences with rocks and then compare their definition with the definition in a dictionary or science book to determine similarities and differences.

Connecting Content: Rocks come in a variety of shapes, textures, and colors; however, they are all made in one of three ways: (1 *igneous* are cooled from molten magma from the Earth's hot interior which erupt onto the surface in volcanoes or intrude into overlying rock; (2 *sedimentary* are made when sediments settle out of water and are then squeezed and cemented until solid; and (3 *metamorphic* are remade from other rocks by the tremendous heat of molten magma or the crushing forces that build mountains.

Making a Model Rock

Materials: pattern page, glue, colored crayons, pencils, or markers

Directions: Explain that the building blocks of rocks are minerals. Tell students that they will use the pattern pieces to make a model showing how minerals make up rocks. Have students color, cut, and glue pattern pieces to make a model of the rock, granite. Then ask them to compare the model to actual granite and describe how they might make a better model.

Connecting Content : The crystals in the igneous rock, granite, are large enough to see individually. This rock solidified gradually from slowly cooling magma in an underground pluton. It has an interlocking crystal texture. The light colored crystals in granite indicate the rock is rich in the minerals quartz and feldspar. The darker crystals are the minerals hornblende and biotite mica. The average granite contains 60% feldspar, 30% quartz, and 10% dark minerals (biotite mica or hornblende). You can extend the activity by having students estimate the percentages of the mineral components of granite. You can also vary the amount of mineral components, deleting some minerals or changing the names of some (identifying feldspar specifically as either orthoclase feldspar or plagioclase feldspar) so that it will be identified as syenite, quartz-diorite, diorite, or gabbro.

Investigating Rocks

Materials: 4 lids, plastic cup of saturated salt water solution, plastic cup of water, eye dropper, hand lens

Directions: Tell students that scientists conduct investigations to find out how rocks form from earth materials. This investigation will determine how the concentration of a mineral in molten earth materials affects the size of the crystals formed when the earth materials cool. Make a saturated salt water solution by adding salt to 1 liter of water until no more salt will dissolve (some of the salt settles out). Then have students follow the directions on the activity sheet adding drops of fresh water and/or salt water to each of the four lids. Allow the liquid to evaporate from the lids overnight and use a hand lens to observe the crystal size the following day. Then ask students to rank the relative size of the crystals from smallest (1) to largest (4).

Connecting Content : Crystal size should increase in direct proportion to salt concentration. Thus, **D** with a 100% concentration should have the largest crystals and **A** with 20% concentration should have the smallest crystal size. Higher salt concentrations produce larger crystals; lower salt concentrations produce smaller crystals. These results are helpful in understanding the formation of pegmatites. Mineral-rich molten magma trapped in the center of a pluton flows into cracks that open into the surrounding granite that is cooling and contracting. This activity demonstrates the link between mineral concentration and crystal size. Because this magma is mineral rich, crystals of exceptional size and beauty solidify in the cracks, forming veins of pegmatite.

OBSERVING ROCKS

Name: _____ Date: _____

1. Observe the rock with a hand lens. List the colors that you see. _____
_____
_____

2. Trace your rock on the graph grid. Color in the shapes and sizes of the particles you observe.

— DRY ROCK —

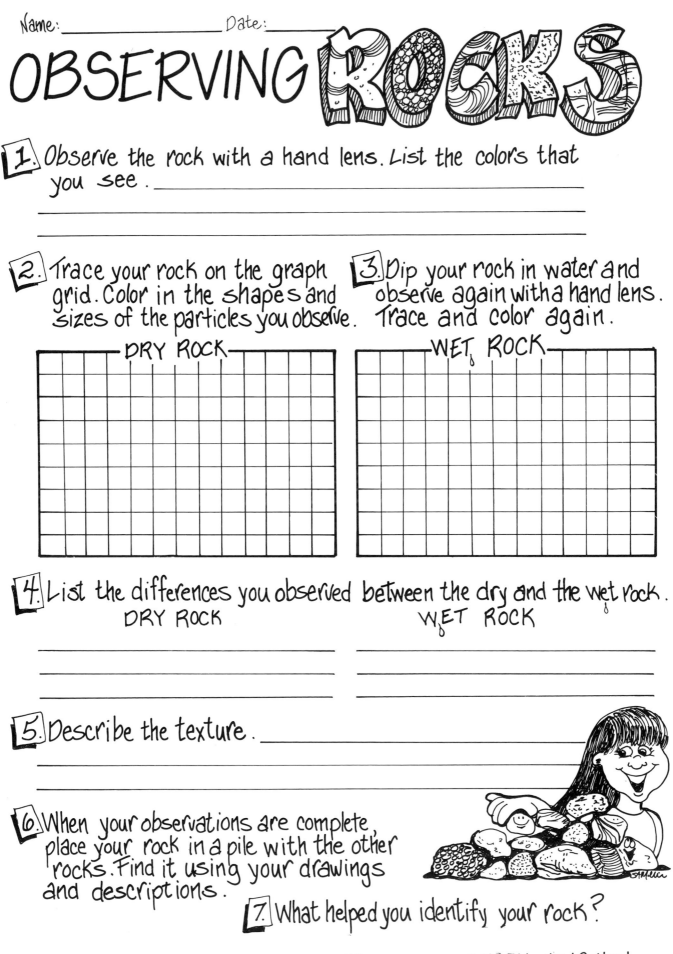

3. Dip your rock in water and observe again with a hand lens. Trace and color again.

— WET ROCK —

4. List the differences you observed between the dry and the wet rock.

DRY ROCK
_____
_____
_____

WET ROCK
_____
_____
_____

5. Describe the texture. _____
_____
_____

6. When your observations are complete, place your rock in a pile with the other rocks. Find it using your drawings and descriptions.

7. What helped you identify your rock?

50   © 1996 Mercier / Ostlund

Name:_____ Date:_____

Communicating about ROCKS

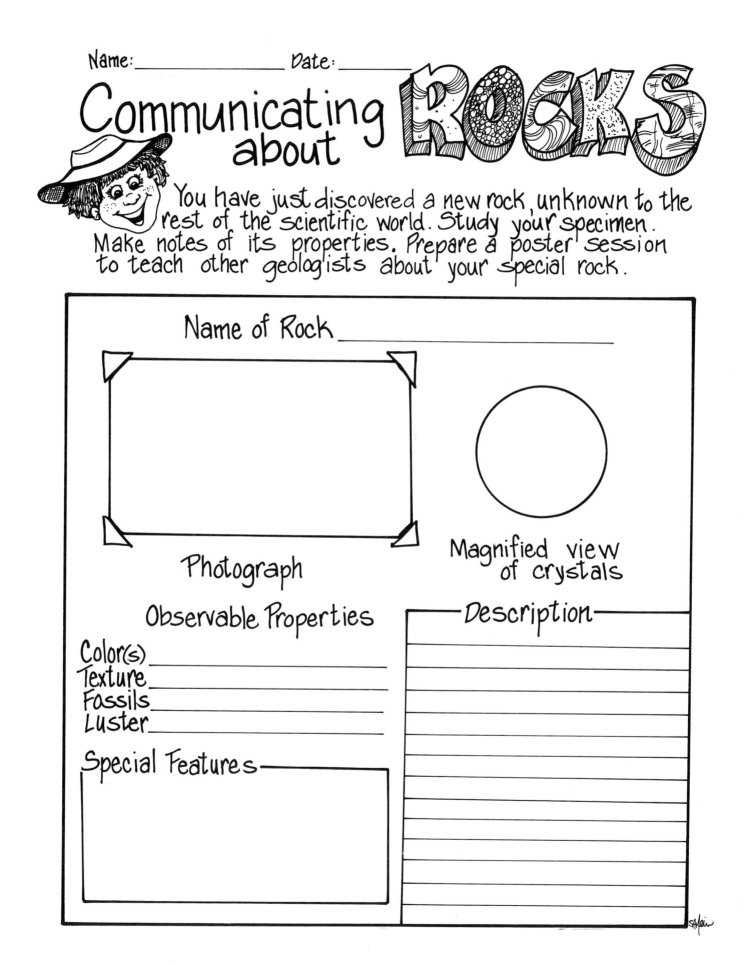

You have just discovered a new rock, unknown to the rest of the scientific world. Study your specimen. Make notes of its properties. Prepare a poster session to teach other geologists about your special rock.

Name of Rock _____

Photograph

Magnified view of crystals

Observable Properties

Color(s) _____
Texture_____
Fossils_____
Luster_____

Special Features

Description

Classifying with ROCKS

1. Observe your set of rocks. Think about their properties. Make a list to use as you classify them.

Properties:

Scientists organize objects and events into groups according to properties.

2. Trace and color your set of rocks in the top box of the chart.

Set of Rocks

3. Divide your set of rocks into 2 groups according to one property of the rocks. Place the groups into the next 2 boxes on the chart. Trace and color to make a record. Label the property.

Set of Rocks

4. Look at the 2 sets of rocks and divide each set into two more groups according to another property. Trace, color and label.

5. Look at the 4 sets of rocks and divide them into 8 sets according to a new property. Trace, color, and label.

6. Explain your classification scheme to a partner scientist.

52

Name: _____

Date: _____

CLASSIFYING with ROCKS

Set of Rocks

Property:

Property:

Property:

Property:

Property:

Property:

P:

P:

P:

P:

P:

P:

P:

P:

Name _____

Date _____

Measuring ROCKS

1. Estimate, measure and record.

	Estimate?		Measurement	
	Rock 1	Rock 2	Rock 1	Rock 2
Length				
Width (widest)				
Width (narrowest)				
Circumference (widest)				
Circumference (narrowest)				
Height from surface				
Mass in grams				
Volume in ml				

2. Draw diagrams of the 2 rocks. Label to show your measurements.

—20cm

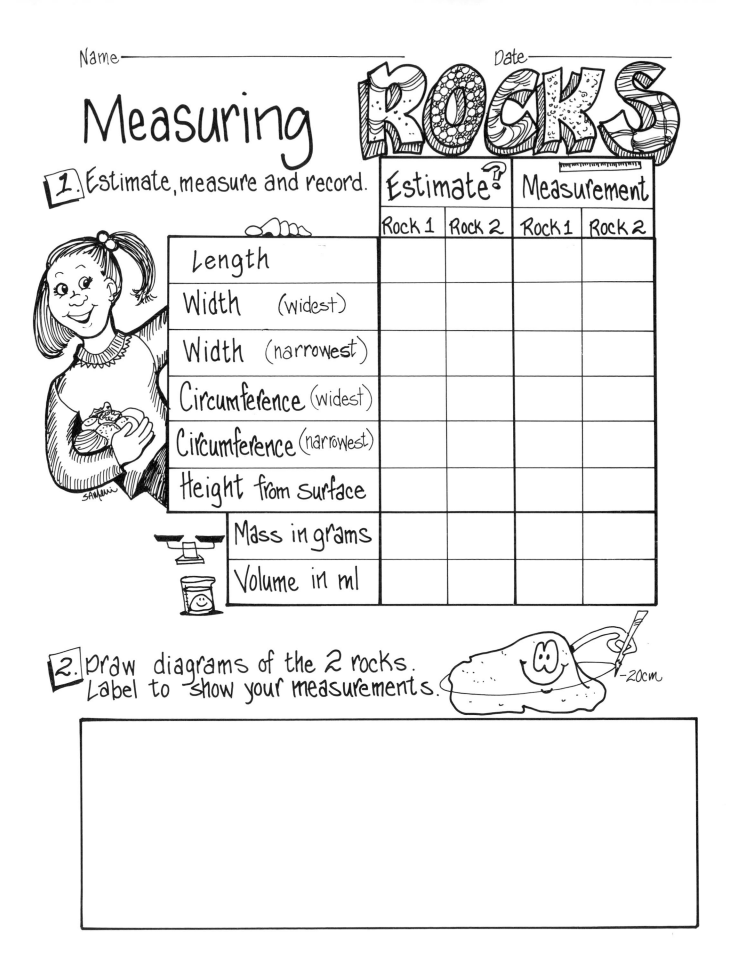

Name_____ Date_____

INFERRING about ROCKS

Rocks are organized into 3 groups according to how they were formed.

METAMORPHIC
form from other rocks when they are transformed by heat, pressure or gain or loss of chemical components

SEDIMENTARY
form by accumulation and compression or cementation of pieces of other rock.

IGNEOUS
form from a molten (melted) state.

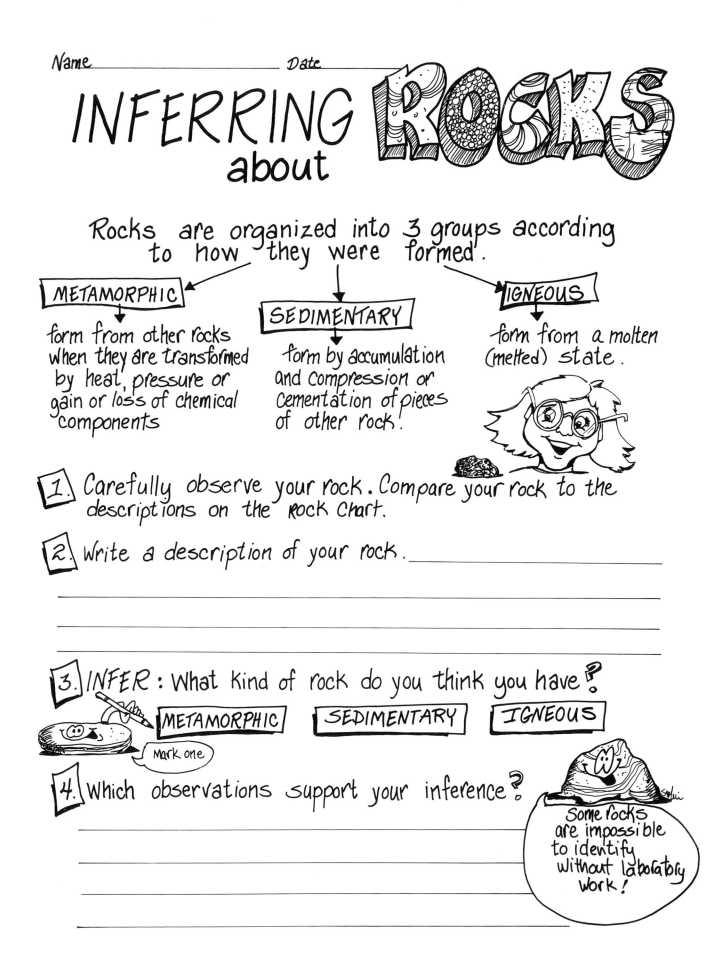

1. Carefully observe your rock. Compare your rock to the descriptions on the rock chart.

2. Write a description of your rock. _____
_____
_____

3. INFER: What kind of rock do you think you have?
   METAMORPHIC   SEDIMENTARY   IGNEOUS
   Mark one

4. Which observations support your inference?
_____
_____
_____
_____

Some rocks are impossible to identify without laboratory work!

ROCK CHART

Compare each description to your rock.
Mark any descriptions that match your rock.

Igneous Rock	Sedimentary Rock	Metamorphic Rock
classified by texture and composition	classified by texture and composition	classified by texture and composition
normally contains no fossils	often contains fossils	rarely has fossils
rarely reacts with acid	may react with acid	may react with acid
usually has no layering	often has bedding usually flat or curved	May have alternate bands of light & dark minerals
usually made of two or more minerals	usually composed of pieces cemented or pressed together	may be composed of only one mineral (marble, quartzite)
may be light or dark colored	has great color variety	may have layers of visible crystals (foliation) or dark & fine grained
usually composed of intergrown mineral crystals which vary in size	may have uniform or variable particle size	usually composed of intergrown mineral crystals which vary in size
sometimes has vesicles (openings) or glass fibers	usually has pores between pieces	rarely has pores or openings
may be fine-grained or glassy (extrusive)	may have cross-bedding, mud cracks, worm burrows, raindrop impressions	may have bent or curved foliation

Name: _____

Date: _____

Predicting with ROCKS

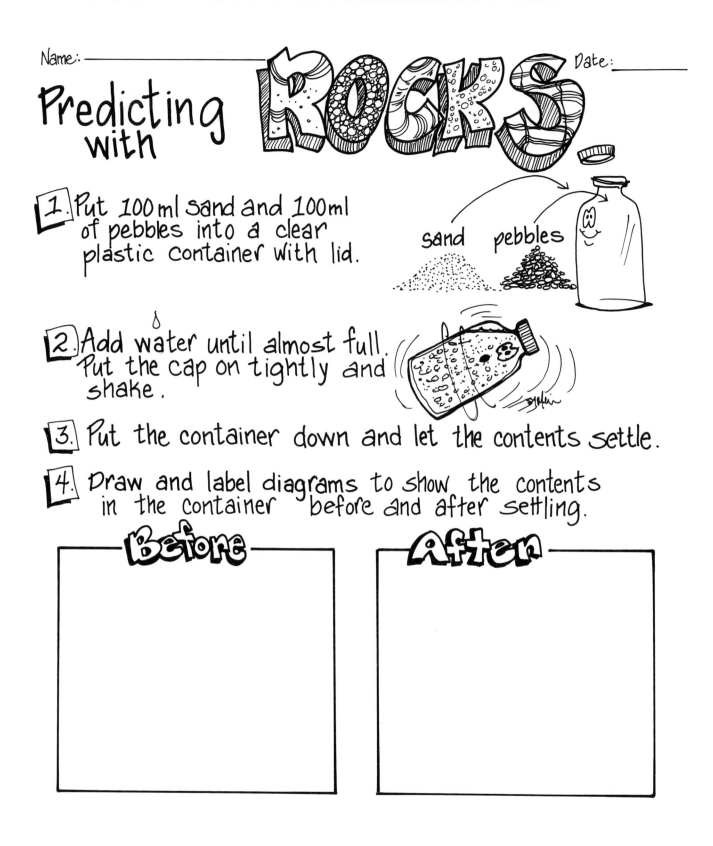

1. Put 100 ml sand and 100ml of pebbles into a clear plastic container with lid.

sand   pebbles

2. Add water until almost full. Put the cap on tightly and shake.

3. Put the container down and let the contents settle.

4. Draw and label diagrams to show the contents in the container before and after settling.

Before

After

5. Explain why you think this happened. _____
_____
_____

Name: _____ Date: _____

Predicting with Rocks   page 2.

6. Put 100 ml sand, 100 ml pebbles and 100 ml of gravel into a container. Add water until almost full.

sand   pebbles   gravel

7. Make a Prediction.
Draw and label a diagram that shows what you think the contents of the container will look like after shaking and settling.

Explain your prediction.
_____
_____
_____
_____
_____
_____

Prediction

8. Shake and let the contents of the container settle. Draw and label a diagram to show the results.

How did your prediction compare with your results?
_____
_____
_____
_____
_____

Results

Name: _____   Date: _____

Defining Operationally

1. Think about all your experiences with rocks. Write a definition of a rock.

_____

_____

_____

2. Use a dictionary or science reference book. Look up the definition of a rock and write it on the lines below.

_____

_____

_____

3. Compare the two definitions.

How are the two alike?	How are the two different?

4. Write a new definition of a rock. _____

_____

_____

© 1996 Mercier / Ostlund

Making a Model ROCK

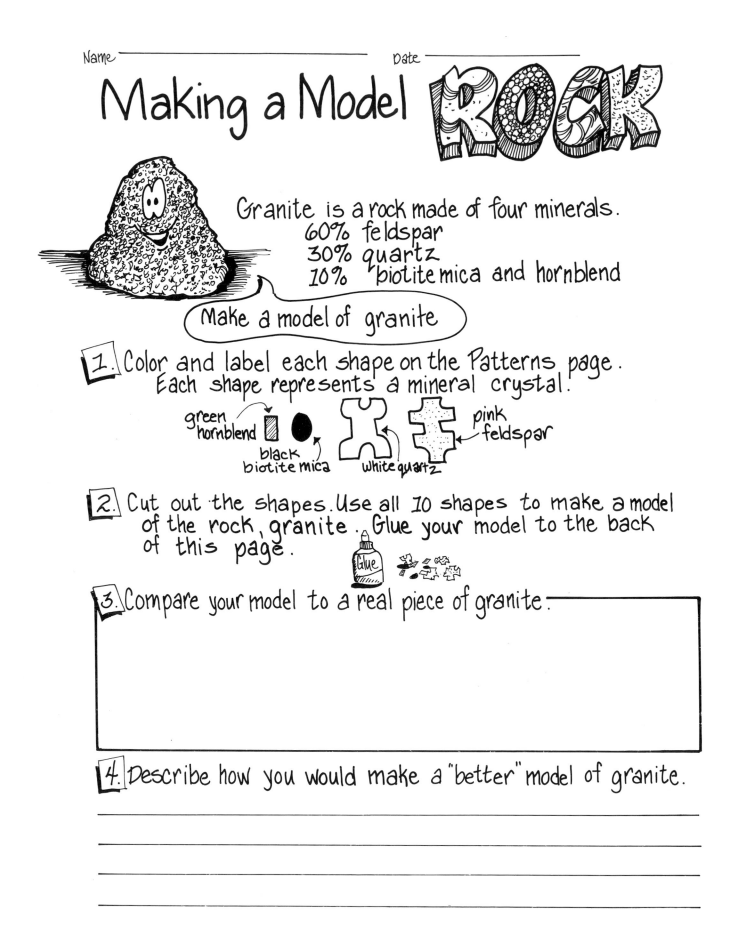

Granite is a rock made of four minerals.
60% feldspar
30% quartz
10% biotite mica and hornblend

Make a model of granite

1. Color and label each shape on the Patterns page. Each shape represents a mineral crystal!

green hornblend
black biotite mica
white quartz
pink feldspar

2. Cut out the shapes. Use all 10 shapes to make a model of the rock, granite. Glue your model to the back of this page.

3. Compare your model to a real piece of granite.

4. Describe how you would make a "better" model of granite.

_____
_____
_____
_____

Making Models of Rocks Patterns

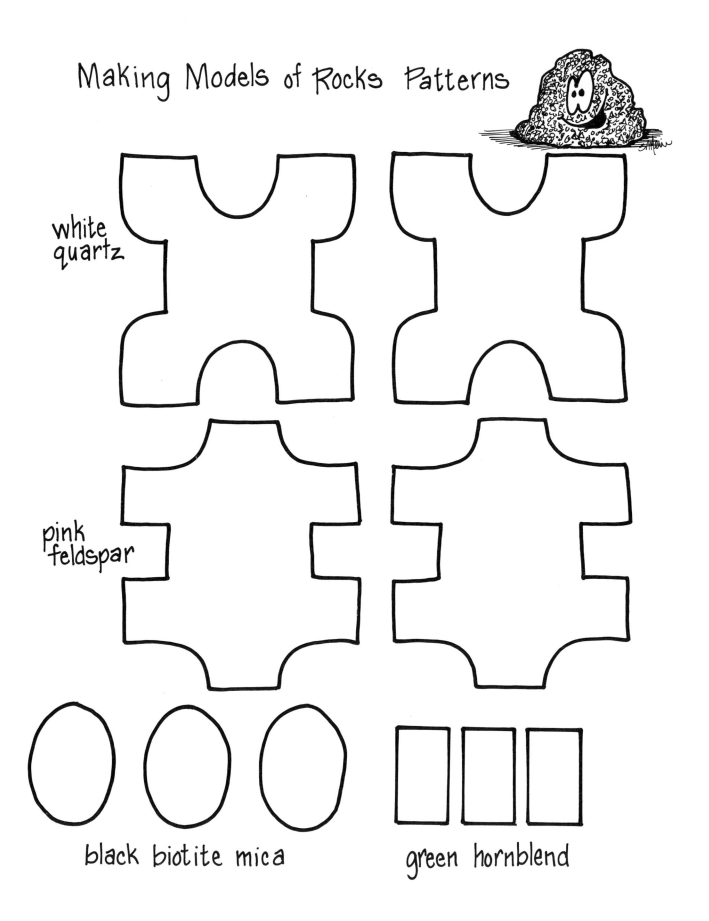

white quartz

pink feldspar

black biotite mica

green hornblend

Name _____   Date _____

Investigating ROCKS

Problem: How does the salt concentration affect crystal size?

Hypothesis: If the salt concentration is greater, then the crystal size will _____

_____

1. Make a saturated solution. Add salt to water until no more will dissolve. 20% 40% 60% 100%

2. Use 4 plastic lids. Label them 20%, 40%, 60%, 100%. Mix the salt water with fresh water as in the chart. Let the water evaporate. Observe and describe the crystals. Hand lens

% Percent salt water concentration

Lid	Salt Solution	Fresh Water	Description of Crystals
20%	20 drops	80 drops	
40%	40 drops	60 drops	
60%	60 drops	40 drops	
100%	100 drops	0 drops	

3. Construct a graph.

Relative crystal size — small → large
4
3
2
1

20% 40% 60% 100%
Percent of salt water concentration

4. What is your conclusion?

_____
_____
_____
_____
_____
_____

Salt is the mineral Halite.

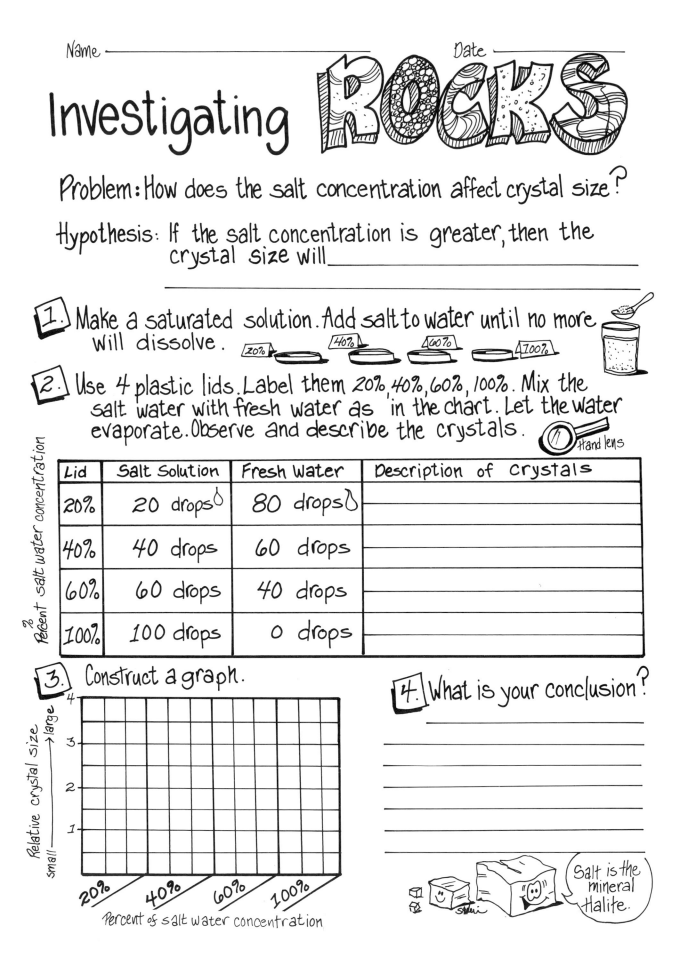

Sound - Making Connections

The Processes of Inquiry / Content Standards

Physical Science Standards:

Levels K-4
- Properties of objects and materials

Levels 5-8
- Properties and changes of properties in matter

In the following activities, students use the processes of inquiry to discover how objects and materials interact with sound energy.

Observing Sound

Materials: empty soda can, pencil

Directions: Ask students if there is a way to make a soda can produce a sound. Then have students use different techniques to produce sounds with a soda can (tapping it with various objects and on different parts of the can, blowing across the hole in the top, etc.) Have students list how they made sounds on the activity sheet in the drawing of the soda can. Then have them list their observations on the bottom of the activity sheet. Point out that when they made a sound with the soda can, they did something that caused the soda can to vibrate.

Connecting Content : Sound is generated whenever an object vibrates and there is a medium such as air to transmit the sound waves. Sound will travel through any substance that returns to its original shape after being disturbed. Sound is transmitted when energetic molecules transfer energy to their neighbors through collisions, and then return to their original positions. Gases, solids, or liquids conduct sound if they transmit compression waves with minimal loss of energy. Sound energy does not travel through a vacuum.

When you play a single note on an instrument you hear a basic note combined with a few higher notes, or overtones, that blend together to give the one note that you hear. When you hit the soda can in the middle, the basic note of the can vibrates more than the overtones, and determines the kind of sound you hear. When you hit the can near the edge, you allow more overtones to blend with the basic note and make a different kind of overall sound. This is something like jumping on a trampoline with another person. If you stand next to a person who is jumping in the middle, you feel very strong vibrations. But if you stand near the edge of the trampoline, the vibrations feel weaker.

Communicating Sound

Materials: *Communicating Sound* handouts, miscellaneous materials for producing sounds (the sound of rain can be produced by making a large cone out of waxed paper and sprinkling salt so it hits the side of the cone; thunder can be produced by shaking a cookie sheet; the sound of ocean waves can be made by putting dried peas into a plastic bowl and slowly tilting it back and forth; the sound of a jet plane can be produced by running a hair dryer at low speed; etc.)

Directions : Make the sound of rain, thunder, ocean waves, or a jet plane and ask students to guess what sound you are producing. Tell students that in this activity they will observe how sounds can communicate different objects and events. Have students cut apart the cards, shuffle, and place them face down. Divide groups of four into two pairs. Then have each pair take turns drawing a card and making the sound on the card while the other member of the pair tries to guess the sound made. *Note: The sound maker and sound guesser are on the same team.* If the first guess is correct the pair scores 5 points, if the second guess is correct 4 points are scored, etc. After five guesses the sound maker should tell the other partner the sound produced. Pairs in each group of four alternate turns.

Connecting Content : Films, radio shows, and plays use sound effects if recordings of real objects and events are not available. Many sound effects can be produced with common objects. The sound waves that enter our ears are interpreted in our brain. Sounds give us all sorts of information about our surroundings. The sounds we make indicate to others that we are happy, sad, angry, or frightened. Sounds, such as a police siren, carry an urgent warning message.

Classifying Sound

Materials: cloth, scissors, paper clip, crayon, straw, can, eraser, book, ruler, pencil

Directions : Ask a student to make a high sound using something in the room. Then ask another student to make a low sound. Ask a student to make a loud sound and a soft sound. Tell students that we interpret the sounds we hear as high or low, loud or soft. Give students the objects listed above and have them drop each object from a height of 10 cm in order to observe and describe the sound each object makes. Suggest that students close their eyes and listen carefully as each object is dropped. Then have them list the objects from loudest sound to softest sound on the first scale. Finally, challenge students to list the objects from highest pitch to lowest pitch on the second scales. Ask students to compare the scales to see if there is any relationship between loudness and the pitch of the sound produced by each object.

Connecting Content : All sounds are produced by the vibrations of material objects. In each case, a vibrating source sends a disturbance through a surrounding medium, usually air, in the form of longitudinal waves. **Loudness** is subjective but is related to sound intensity. It is a measure of the amount of energy in the sound - the more energy, the louder the sound. More energy means more molecules of air (or other medium) get put into motion. You can say that the loudness of a sound is determined by the intensity of the vibrations that cause it. The relative amount of energy in sounds is measured in *decibels*. A whisper is about 50 decibels and a jet plane taking off is about 120 decibels.

The sound **pitch** (highness or lowness) is directly proportional to its vibrational frequency. Frequency is an objective measure of how rapidly something is vibrating. Pitch, is an interpretation of frequency by the listener. Pitch depends on the number of vibrations that reach the ear every second. The greater the number of vibrations that reach the ear every second, the higher the pitch. Hertz (Hz) refers to the number of vibrations in a second. A 50 Hz sound comes from a source that is vibrating 50 times a second.

Measuring with Sound

Materials: 4 straws, scissors, tape, ruler

Directions : Give each student 4 straws. Challenge each student to cut the straws resulting in 7 straws of different lengths with no pieces left over. Then have them tape the straws in order according to length, blow across the tops of the straws and compare the pitch of the sounds produced to determine the length of the straw that produces the highest pitch and the length of the straw that makes the lowest pitch. Then have students measure each straw.

Connecting Content : The shorter the straw, then the higher the pitch produced (the more frequently the air inside the straw vibrates). The longer the straw, then the lower the pitch produced (the less frequently the air inside vibrates). The general rule is, the shorter the object, the higher the pitch.

Inferring Sound

Materials: partially fill 10 numbered film canisters with different objects (i.e., rice, coins, dried beans, miniature marshmallows, spool of thread, screws, bolts, rubber bands, balls of aluminum foil, macaroni or shell pasta, buttons, etc.) Note: Make a set of 10 film canisters for each group of four and put each set in a resealable plastic bag.

Directions : Shake one of the film canisters and invite students to infer what might be inside. Ask students to explain how the sound they heard lead them to the inference they made about what was inside the canister. Then give each group of four a set of 10 film canisters partially filled with different objects. Ask students to shake each canister ad observe the sound produced. Have them infer and draw what is inside each canister on the activity sheet. Then have them open each canister and circle the inferences that were correct. Finally, ask them the explain how shaking the canisters helped them infer the object(s) inside.

Connecting Content : The ability to identify sounds and tell sound apart is called sound discrimination. Objects vibrate at their own unique natural frequencies, allowing us to differentiate one from another. **The natural (resonant) frequency is the frequency at which the least amount of energy is necessary to cause the object to vibrate.** It is dependent upon the object's shape and elasticity and is largely responsible for the characteristic sounds associated with the object. Each wire in a piano, or each piece of metal in a xylophone has a specific natural frequency, and therefore produces a specific note.

Predicting with Sound

Materials: 5 film canisters, dried beans

Directions : Ask students to guess how many beans a film canister can hold. Then shake a film canister that is full of beans and another film canister that 1/4 full of beans. Ask students how the sound differs between the two canisters. Tell students that they should guess the number of beans in a full film canister and then actually count the beans. Then ask students to put different amounts of beans in five film canisters, put the lid on, shake the canister, and describe how the sound differs with different amounts of beans. Divide each group of four into two pairs. Then have one member of the pair count out beans, put the beans in five canisters, and have the partner shake the canisters in order to predict the number of beans in each one.

Connecting Content : The more beans packed together in a film canister, the less the beans are free to vibrate and produce a sound when you shake the canister. However, if there are fewer beans in the canister, they are free to vibrate and produce sound when you shake it. Therefore, the loudness and pitch of the sound produced can indicate how many beans are in the canister. The louder and higher the pitch of the sound produced, the fewer beans are in the canister. (See **Communicating** for background information about loudness and pitch.)

Defining Operationally

Materials: pictures or actual musical instruments

Directions : Explain that a sound wave is an organized disturbance. To illustrate this point, create a wave in the room. Have one student, at the edge of the room, stand up and then quickly sit down. Immediately, the person next to the first stands and sits and the chain reaction continues across the room. Stress the fact that a wave is not something made of matter, but rather the movement of energy.

Ask students how a sound wave is produced by different objects. Optional: Show a picture or an actual string instrument. Explain that instruments with strings have a hollow box underneath the strings. The vibrations of the strings make the air inside the box vibrate. This, in turn, makes the air around the box vibrate. Display a woodwind or brass instrument. Explain that by blowing in the instrument, the air inside vibrates to produce sound. Exhibit a percussion instrument. Explain that a sound is produced by striking the instrument. Then have students find an object that produces sound, draw a diagram to illustrate how sound is produced by the object, and operationally define a sound producing object.

Connecting Content : Sound is generated whenever an object vibrates and there is a medium such as air to transmit the sound waves. Sound is a wave phenomenon, transmitting energy but *not* matter. For example, two people can sit on opposite sides of a campfire and talk to each other through the smoke without the smoke moving one direction or the other. Compression waves move through air, smoke, steel, or other media without transporting the media itself.

When a door is opened into a room, a pulse of pressurized (compressed) air moves across the room and may push curtains out an open window on the other side. A pulse of depressurized (rarefied) air is produced when the door closes, and the air outside the window pushes the curtains back into the room. If the door is repeatedly opened and closed, waves of compressed and rarefied air resembling sound waves are formed. **Sound is a series of compression and rarefaction waves.** Figure A shows how the expanding tongs of a tuning fork compress air, while Figure B shows how the retracting tongs leave a partial vacuum behind them. If the tuning fork is allowed to vibrate, a series of compression and rarefaction waves is established, as shown in Figure C. The wavelength of the resulting sound is the distance between successive rarefactions or compressions. If you put your hand next to the "woofer" (base membrane) of a stereo speaker you can actually feel the compression waves as they impact you hand.

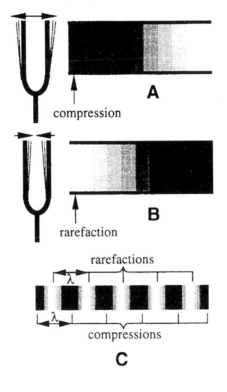

Making Models with Sound

Materials: a variety of materials such as toilet paper tubes, plastic soda bottles cut off 3 cm from the top to make a funnel, string, balloons, cans, etc.; optional: overhead of activity sheet

Directions : Go over the diagram of the ear on the activity sheet (Optional: Use an overhead of the activity sheet). Explain how each part of the ear works (See Connecting Content (below). Ask students to suggest objects that could be used to represent each part of the ear and give a rationale for why each object would be a good representation for each ear part. Then ask students to construct a model of the ear, draw and label an illustration of their models, and provide a reason for why they chose each object to represent each part of the ear.

Connecting Content : When you hear a sound, sound waves are collected by your outer ear and travel down a small tube, called the ear canal, to your eardrum. When the sound waves reach your eardrum, the eardrum vibrates. The vibrating eardrum pushes against three tiny bones: the hammer, anvil, and stirrup. The bones make the vibrations louder. The stirrup pushes against a coiled tube filled with liquid. The tube, or cochlea, is lined with thousands of tiny hairs. When sound waves make the liquid move, the hairs wave back and forth. These moving hairs are connected to nerves that carry the sound message to your brain.

Investigating Sound

Materials : 8 bottles, water, pencil, straw

Directions : Divide class into groups of four. Give each group of four 8 bottles, water, and a pencil. Challenge groups to fill the bottles with water so each one produces a different note resulting in a scale of 8 notes. Have students draw an measure the water in each bottle. Ask students how they can figure out how much air is in each bottle. (Fill one bottle completely with water, measure the amount of water, and subtract the amount of water in each bottle from the amount of water in a completely full bottle.) Have students graph the amount of water and air in the bottles using different colors for each graph. Then have them blow across the bottles using a straw (to insure sanitary conditions). Ask students to compare the results of tapping and blowing across the bottles with the pitch of the sound produced. Ask students to draw a conclusion about how the water affects the pitch of the sound produced by tapping or blowing across the bottles.

Connecting Content : When you tap the bottles, you make the water vibrate. The bottles with the smallest amount of water produces the highest note, and the bottles with the most water produces the lowest note. When you blow across the top of a bottle, the air inside the bottle vibrates. The more air in the bottle, the slower it vibrates and the lower the sound. The bottle with the least amount of water (and the most air) has the lowest sound.

The scientific study of Sound is Acoustics.

SOUND

Waves A wave carries energy from one place to another. A wave does not carry material. Sound is energy made from vibrating objects. The mechanical energy of sound travels in waves as it moves through solids, liquids, and gases away from the vibrating object. Sound cannot travel through a vacuum.

Vibration When you pluck the string of a guitar, the elastic wave travels to the end of the string and bounces to travel back and forth the full length of the string making a vibration. The wood begins to vibrate at the same rate, which causes the air to vibrate in sound waves that we can hear.

Pitch Pitch is the degree of highness or lowness of the sound as heard by the listener. An object that vibrates quickly has a higher pitch of sound as an object that vibrates slowly. Smaller objects vibrate faster than larger ones.

Loudness The loudness of sound is how strong the sound seems to us when it strikes our ears. Loud sounds have more energy than soft sounds. Waves spread out from the source in all directions like waves from a pebble in a pond. The loudness decreases as you get farther away from the source.

Hearing Sound is around us all the time. The air makes it possible for us to communicate with each other by speaking and hearing. The human ear has an eardrum which vibrates with sound waves. These vibrations cause vibrations in a chain of 3 bones, the hammer, anvil and stirrup. The bones act like a lever so that the stirrup sends stronger vibrations to the cochlea. There is fluid inside the cochlea which vibrates and cells inside the cochlea change the vibrations to electric signals. These electric signals travel the auditory nerve to the brain. The brain interprets these signals as sound.

bone, eardrum, Anvil, bone, Hammer, Cochlea, Stirrup, Nerve

Name _____ Date _____

OBSERVING SOUND

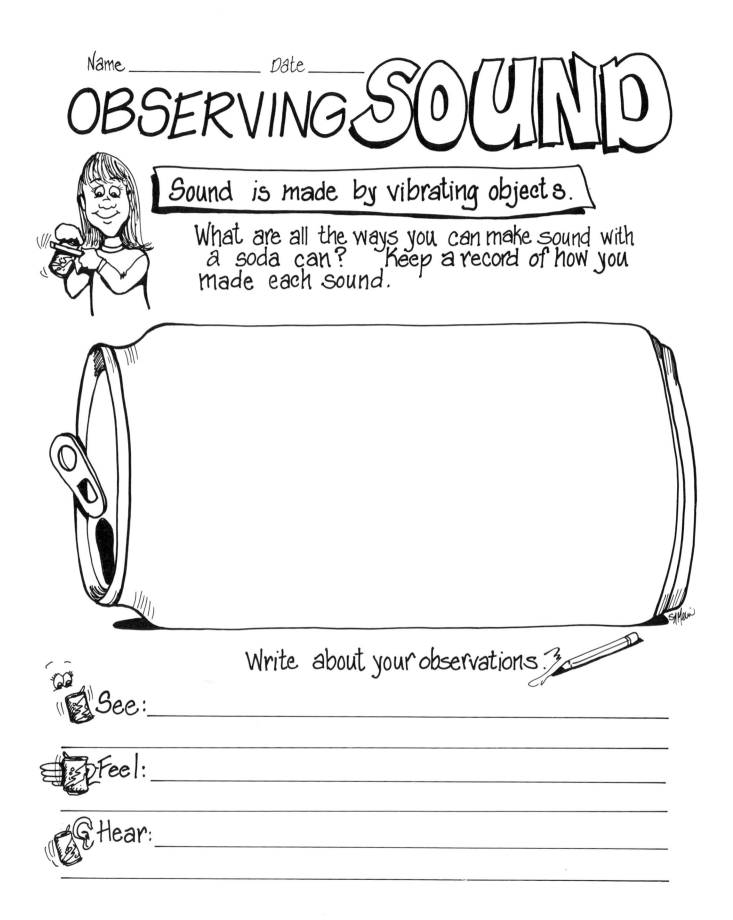

Sound is made by vibrating objects.

What are all the ways you can make sound with a soda can? Keep a record of how you made each sound.

Write about your observations.

See: _____
_____

Feel: _____
_____

Hear: _____
_____

Name:_____ Date:_____

Communicating SOUND

You have 1 minute to help your partner guess your sound. No talking allowed! Use your mouth, body or other objects to help you communicate the sound.

1. Draw a card, make the sound. Have your partner guess.
2. Make a record, 5 points for correct guesses.
3. Teams take turns for 20 rounds.

	Team ONE	Player:_____ Player:_____			Team TWO	Player:_____ Player:_____	
	Name of Sound	How Produced	Points		Name of Sound	How Produced	Points
1.				2.			
3.				4.			
5.				6.			
7.				8.			
9.				10.			
11.				12.			
13.				14.			
15.				16.			
17.				18.			
19.				20.			

4. What helped you identify the sounds?

72   © 1996 Mercier / Ostlund

Communicating Sound - Cut apart the cards, shuffle and place face down. Players draw a card and try to make the sound while partner guesses.

Horse running	Dog growling	Monkey	Opening and pouring soda
Cat purring	Scratching an itch	Wolf howling	Rainstorm
Blowing nose	Clock ticking	Coins Dropping	Squeaking door closing
Drummer in a band	Doorbell	Mosquito	Violin
Leaky faucet	Electric Guitar	Train	Heartbeat _Thump Thump_
Popcorn popping	Ocean Waves	Car motor	Writing with a pencil
Popping Bubblegum	Airplane	Person running away	Frog hopping

Classifying SOUND

1. Drop each object from a 10cm height. Observe and describe the sound each one makes.

Object	Description of Sound	Object	Description of Sound
cloth		can	
scissors		eraser	
paper clip		book	
crayon		ruler	
straw		pencil	

2. Seriate the sounds. Place them on a scale of 1-10.

Loudest Sound | 10 9 8 7 6 5 4 3 2 1 | Softest Sound

Highest Pitch | 10 9 8 7 6 5 4 3 2 1 | Lowest Pitch

3. How do your two scales compare?_____

_____

Measuring with SOUND

1. You have 4 straws. Your challenge is to cut them so that you have 7 straws of different lengths with no pieces left over.

Trace and Measure Your Straws Below ↘

2.

3. Cut a piece of tape 12cm long. Lay your straws on the tape with the longest straw at one end and the shortest straw at the other. Put tape across the top.

4. Blow across the tops of the straws. Listen to sounds.

Measure straw with highest note _____ cm
Measure straw with lowest note _____ cm

5. Measure the straws in order from highest pitch sound to lowest pitch sound. Record measurements below.

cm	cm	cm	cm	cm	cm	cm

Highest ————————————————→ Lowest
Pitch   Pitch

INFERRING SOUND

1. Shake each container and observe the sound produced.

2. Infer and draw what you think is inside each one.

1.	2.	3.	4.	5.
6.	7.	8.	9.	10.

3. Open each container and circle the number of inferences that were correct.

4. Explain how shaking the containers helped you infer the object inside.

_____

_____

_____

_____

_____

_____

Name ———————— Date ———————

Predicting with SOUND

1. Fill a film canister with beans. Make a guess of how many beans it holds when full.

Guess ————— Count —————

2. Test by putting in different amounts of beans. Shake the canister and observe. Describe the differences.

Number of beans	Description

3. Work with a partner. Count out some beans. Put them in the canister. Have your partner shake it and predict how many beans are inside. Compute the difference. Take turns.

Trial	Prediction # ❤	Real Count # ❤	Difference
1.			
2.			
3.			
4.			
5.			

4. Explain how you made your predictions

© 1996 Mercier / Ostlund

Name: _____ Date: _____

Defining Operationally

1. Find an object that produces sound.

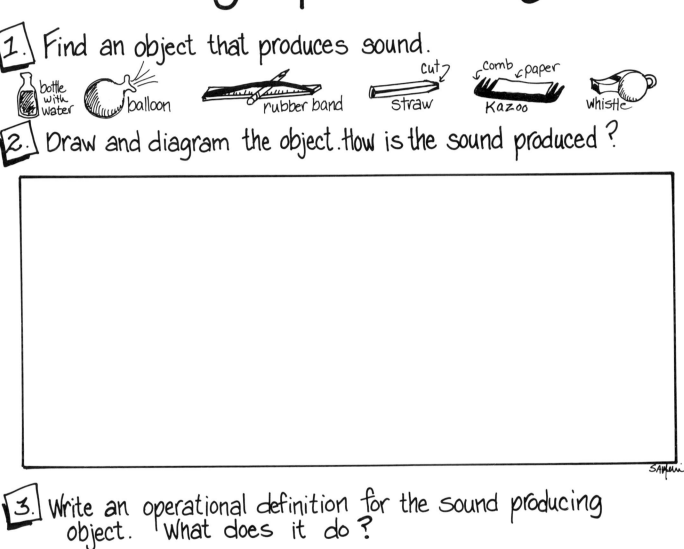

bottle with water   balloon   rubber band   straw   cut →   comb → paper   Kazoo   whistle

2. Draw and diagram the object. How is the sound produced?

3. Write an operational definition for the sound producing object. What does it do?

_____

_____

_____

_____

_____

_____

Name:_____ Date:_____

Making Models with SOUND

Auricle catches sound waves

vibrates with sound waves
Ear Drum

Semicircular Canals for balance

Nerve to Brain

Sound Waves

Ear Canal

Cochlea fluid inside

3 Bones
Malleus, Incus, Staples

Eustacian Tube to the throat

1. Think about how your ear works. Look around for objects that you could use to represent different parts of the ear.

2. Draw your model design and label.

3. Explain why you chose each object. _____

_____

_____

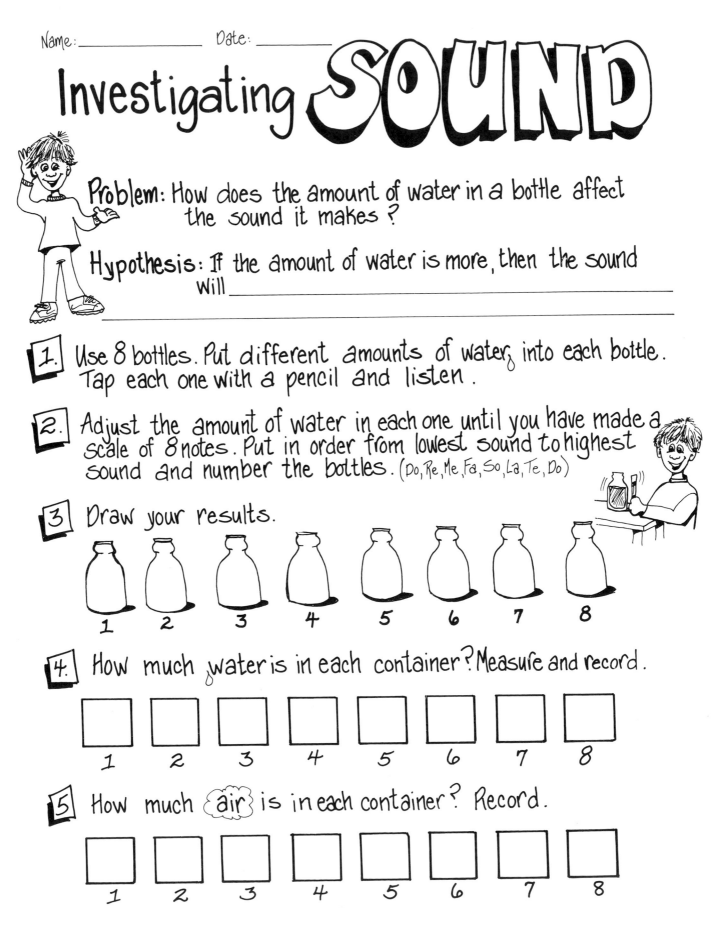

Name: _____ Date: _____

Investigating SOUND

Problem: How does the amount of water in a bottle affect the sound it makes?

Hypothesis: If the amount of water is more, then the sound will _____

1. Use 8 bottles. Put different amounts of water into each bottle. Tap each one with a pencil and listen.

2. Adjust the amount of water in each one until you have made a scale of 8 notes. Put in order from lowest sound to highest sound and number the bottles. (Do, Re, Me, Fa, So, La, Te, Do)

3. Draw your results.

   1   2   3   4   5   6   7   8

4. How much water is in each container? Measure and record.

   1   2   3   4   5   6   7   8

5. How much air is in each container? Record.

   1   2   3   4   5   6   7   8

6. Communicate your data in two graphs.

Water

Amount of water — Bottle Number — 1 2 3 4 5 6 7 8

Air

Amount of air — Bottle Number — 1 2 3 4 5 6 7 8

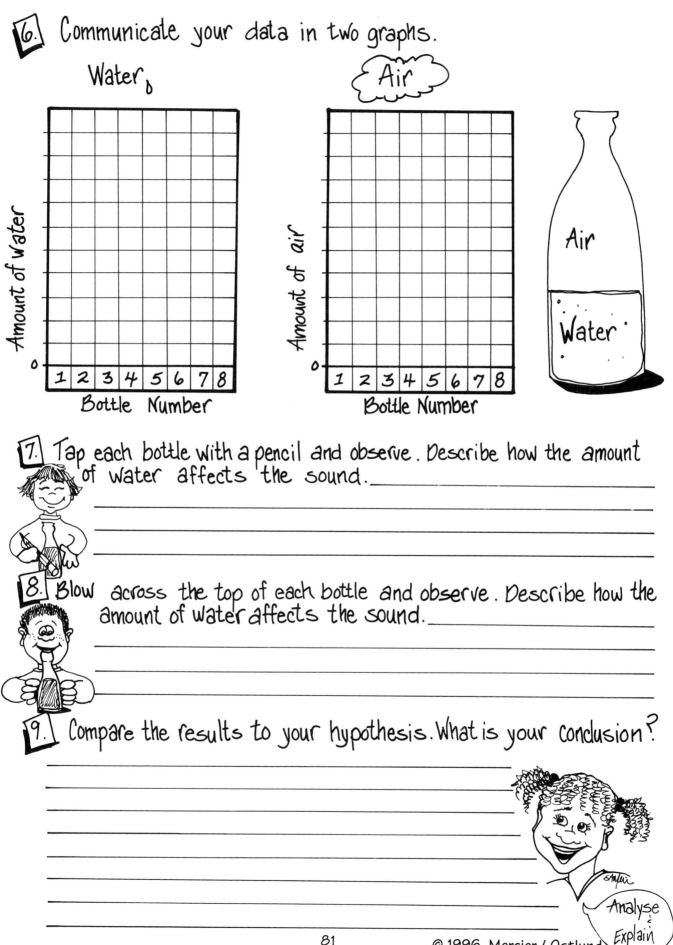

Air

Water

7. Tap each bottle with a pencil and observe. Describe how the amount of water affects the sound. _____
_____
_____
_____

8. Blow across the top of each bottle and observe. Describe how the amount of water affects the sound. _____
_____
_____
_____

9. Compare the results to your hypothesis. What is your conclusion?
_____
_____
_____
_____
_____
_____
_____

Analyse & Explain

81   © 1996 Mercier / Ostlund

PUTTING IT ALL TOGETHER:
A SCIENCE FAIR PROJECT

The National Science Education Standards challenge us to provide experiences in science that actively engage students in construction of ideas and explanations about the world around them. These experiences must develop their abilities to do scientific inquiry and deepen their understandings about how science is done. The activities and investigations in this book provide opportunities for students to develop and apply the scientific inquiry processes that are needed to carry out a scientific study.

Science Fair competitions provide opportunities for students to carry out in-depth investigations on science topics of their choice. Science Fairs are challenging and can be overwhelming to teachers, students, and parents. Use the following pages to guide students towards the completion of a Science Fair Project. The template can be used to design a mini science fair board as a practice to their real study. It is the right size to cut out and arrange on a 12" x 18" piece of colored construction paper. Many of the activities presented in <u>RISING TO THE CHALLENGE</u> could be extended into investigations that meet local Science Fair expectations and regulations.

PUTTING IT ALL TOGETHER:
A SCIENCE FAIR PROJECT

Title: Write a name for your investigation

Problem: State the problem or describe the problem to study.

Question: State the problem in the form of a question.

Hypothesis: Write an if... then... statement that explains what you think will happen in your investigation.

Experiment Design: Explain the steps you are going to take to investigate your question. Tell what you will change and what you will measure. Variables:
    1. Manipulated (what you will change)
    2. Responding (what you measure)
    3. Controlled (what stays the same)

Results : Analyze your data. Think about the evidence you collected. Explain how your findings answer your question.

Conclusion: Compare your results to your hypothesis. Tell if your results support or refute your hypothesis.

Research: Search the library and other data sources to find the current scientific knowledge about this topic or problem.

Materials : Make a list of the materials used in your investigation.

Pictures/ Diagrams : Draw diagrams or take photos to show your results.

Data Collected: Make systematic observations. Take accurate measurements. Organize the data into tables and charts.

Data Display : Show the collected data in a graph.

Title

Problem

Question

Hypothesis

Experiment Design

Results

Conclusion

Aha!

Research

Data Collected

Materials

Pictures/Diagrams

Data Display
Graph Title:

Assessment Strategies

Daily Self-Assessment

Self-assessment involves students in reflecting and reporting on their own performance and attitudes. It can take many forms- from journal entries and student writings to questionnaires and rating scales. No matter what form it takes, self-assessment is of most value if the students feel comfortable enough to be honest about their own strengths and needs for improvement without fear of being penalized for this insight. If students have not had much previous experience with self-assessment, you may wish to provide a model by evaluating your own performance. The following questions can be used to prompt self-assessment:

- What did you accomplish today?
- What strengths do you think you showed in your work? What things would you like to improve?
- How did you feel about the topic we investigated today?
- How well do you think you understood the activity we did today?
- What questions do you have about what we did today? Are there some things you don't understand?
- What topics would you like to investigate tomorrow?
- What do you feel is the most important thing you learned in science this week?

Portfolios

A portfolio is a sampling of a student's work selected over a period of time, such as a semester or a year. It gives a picture of the quality of a student's work, and of the growth and change in a student's scientific capabilities.

What Belongs in a Portfolio?

The contents of a portfolio usually meet criteria such as:

- **The work should be significant and interesting.** This will vary greatly among students. For some it means the results of a complex project. For other it may be a simple assignment completed perfectly for the first time.
- **The student should want it in the portfolio.** The portfolio represents, among other things, what the student thinks is his or her most representative work.
- **The portfolio should cover as long a time span as possible.** This assures that the portfolio can show growth and change in the student's scientific capabilities.
- **The portfolio should contain from six to ten entries.** One difference between a cumulative folder and a portfolio is the selection process. A portfolio includes thoughtfully selected entries chosen to satisfy the requirements listed above.

Evaluating Portfolios

Portfolios evaluated by students and parents help both to understand the students' progress. Your evaluations give you further perspective into how your class is progressing, as well as a chance to reflect on your own program.

Observation Checklists

A checklist that specifies science process skills and cooperative/collaborative group social skills can to used to record observations of students while they work in small groups. The way in which you evaluate your students' work will tell your students what you value. If, for example, you focus only on their getting facts correct, students will learn to downplay process, organization, and creativity. Determine the appropriate focus, then select the scoring approach most suitable for your needs.

- Score **S** and **U** (or **1** and **0**) for each focus of the student's work that is satisfactory or unsatisfactory.
- Score **S, A**. and **U** (or **2, 1**, and **0**) for each focus of the student's work that is satisfactory, acceptable, or unsatisfactory.
- Score from **4** to **1**, with **4** being excellent, **3** good, **2** satisfactory, and **1** needs improvement.

Sample Checklist

Observe a Shell	
1. Process Skill (*Observing*): Does the student carefully look at the shell to distinguish its features?	
2. Social Skill (*Listen to Others*): Does the student listen when the partner tells about his or her shell?	
Communicating about Shells	
1. Process Skill (*Communicating*): Do the student's drawings and descriptions accurately convey the properties of the shell, including size, color, and shape?	
2. Social Skill (*Disagree in an Agreeable Way*): Does the student disagree respectfully with other about which shell they used to communicate?	
Classifying with Shells	
1. Process Skill (*Classifying*): Does the student attempt to distinguish among the shells?	
2. Social Skill (*Explain and Summarize*): Can the student accurately explain and summarize the steps their group took to classify the shells?	
Inferring with Shells	
1. Process Skill (*Inferring*): Can the student infer what the shell looked like from the broken piece of shell?	
2. Social Skill (*Encourage and Respect Others*): Does the student treat his or her group members with respect while completing the activity?	
Making Models	
1. Process Skill (*Making Models*): Does the student construct an accurate physical representation of a shell with modeling compound?	
2. Social Skill (*Check for Understanding*): Does the student ask group members about how their models differ from an actual shell?	

Performance Tasks

The following rubrics are guidelines for assessing performance tasks. They are divided into four levels which are easy to use and provide a reasonable amount of discrimination. Commercial or state-prepared performance assessment instruments often use a 5-, 6-, or 7-point scale to make sharper distinctions. These instruments are typically used annually, not with the frequency of daily, weekly performance task assessments.

Performance assessments which incorporate a variety of methods such as paper-and-pencil tasks, projects, and manipulative experiences should include the following criteria:

- **The work or activity that the student performs is authentic.** Open-ended situations are presented in which there may be no clear answer or multiple possibilities.

- **The work is often varied in methods used and in the way results are presented.** Students may be given a task such as:
  - Draw or write your observations about...
  - Make a chart to show...
  - Describe how...
  - Compare and contrast...
  - Give examples of...
  - Explain the difference between...

- **The student usually needs to display communication skills.** Questions often include the requirement that students justify their work. It is appropriate to consider how well the student presents information; however, if a student displays understanding and obtains good answers, that should weigh more than how results are communicated. In other words, students should not be penalized for their lack of English proficiency.

- **Evaluation of the work is often multidimensional.** Performance assessment usually indicates a more complex task than is found on ordinary tests. It is useful to have established criteria (a scoring rubric) by which to students' work is evaluated.

RUBRIC

4	Full accomplishment	• Student correctly performs the activity. • Student accurately describes the object or event, using different senses. • Student can identify the senses used to describe the object or event. • Student contributes new ideas to describe the object or event.
3	Substantial accomplishment	• Student follows directions to perform the activity. • Student accurately describes the object or event, using different senses. • Student cannot identify which senses were used or cannot contribute new ideas to describe the object or event.
2	Partial accomplishment	• Student follows directions to perform the activity. • Student uses inappropriate words to describe the object or event or cannot identify what senses were used.
1	Little or no progress toward accomplishment	• Student misunderstands the activity or makes little or no effort to participate.

Advanced RUBRIC

4	Full accomplishment	Student applies appropriate skills, concepts, and techniques; communicates the results using appropriate means (writing, diagrams, graphs, non-paper-and-pencil media); and justifies or explains the results as appropriate to the task.
3	Substantial accomplishment	Student uses appropriate science skills, but may make a few simple errors in computation, or recording data. Student indicates an understanding of the appropriate concepts, communication is good, but could be stronger, clearer, or more complete.
2	Partial accomplishment	The results are inadequately reported. Student gives an incomplete and/or erroneous response. Student appears to have a limited grasp of the concept or science skills, does not address the conditions of the situation, or may not use logical reasoning.
1	Little or no progress toward accomplishment	Student does not use science skills or apply concept. Student does not attempt performance task.